quick & easy chinese

quick & easy chinese

70 everyday recipes

by **Nancie McDermott**   *photographs by* Maren Caruso

CHRONICLE BOOKS
SAN FRANCISCO

Dedication:
To the memory of Dr. Ting-Chien Lee, (1923–1985).
Through his work as a pediatrician, scientist, scholar,
and teacher, he made this world a better place. Through
his example as a son, brother, husband, father, and
friend, he showed his family and community how to
live with generosity, wisdom, and love.

�

Acknowledgments:
Ten thousand thanks to the brilliant team at Chronicle
Books: Bill LeBlond and Amy Treadwell who said "yes"
and saw things through with patient wisdom; Peter Perez
and Amy Portello who put my books into the limelight
and kept them there; and Jennifer Tolo Pierce whose
extraordinarily beautiful design illuminates this book.
Photographer Maren Caruso and her team brought the
recipes to life handsomely through their excellent work.
Sarah Baurle, Jane Falla, and my literary agent Lisa
Ekus-Saffer continue to work thoughtfully and tirelessly
on my behalf. My beloved friends Jill O'Connor, Dean
Nichols, and Debbie Gooch keep me laughing and looking
ahead, and my husband Will Lee and daughters Camellia
and Isabelle feed my heart and soul every single day.

Text copyright © 2008 by Nancie McDermott.

Photographs copyright © 2008 by Maren Caruso.

Library of Congress Cataloging-in-Publication Data
McDermott, Nancie.
Quick and easy Chinese / by Nancie McDermott.
        p. cm.
Includes bibliographical references.
ISBN 978-0-8118-5930-1 (alk. paper)
1. Cookery, Chinese. 2. Quick and easy cookery. I. Title.
TX724.5.C5M3534 2008
641.5'55—dc22
                        2007042028

ISBN: 978-0-8118-5930-1

Manufactured in China.

Designed by Jennifer Tolo Pierce

Food and prop styling: Kim Konecny
Food styling assistant: Julia Scahill
Photo assistants: Scott Mansfield and Faiza Ali

10 9 8 7 6 5 4

Chronicle Books LLC
680 Second Street
San Francisco, California 94107

www.chroniclebooks.com

TABLE OF CONTENTS

INTRODUCTION

It's another way-beyond-busy weeknight, and all across the land, many a would-be cook reaches out for two things: the telephone and the take-out menu for ordering Chinese. It's fast, handy, satisfying, and more varied than pizza, and if you're lucky, it can be delivered to your door.

We enjoy going out to eat Chinese food too, whether we're seated in a local mom-and-pop restaurant, a glittering dim sum palace, or a plush temple of haute cuisine *Chinoise*. Chinese takeout fills us up at lunch and dinner and serves as a mealtime staple on the way home from work. Enamored of delicacies such as won ton soup, *mu shu* pork, *kung pao* chicken, and orange beef, and blessed with abundant and varied sources for it, we are a people in love with Chinese food.

Our appreciation for Chinese food is so strong that a new generation of Chinese eateries has joined the marketplace in the last decade, serving up a Chinese-inspired take on fast food. Visit the food court at any major shopping mall or airport, and you'll find multiple counters serving generous portions of dishes many Chinese people would not recognize. Meat and veggies are napped in delightfully flavorful sauces, creating delicious hybrids that we mall rats love. Major upscale chain restaurants are thriving as well, some serving pan-Asian menus and others offering their version of traditional Chinese cuisine.

Clearly we love Chinese food, and we partake of it in its various incarnations all across the land. The place we need to see it next is on our own kitchen tables. Wonderful Chinese dishes belong among the basic weeknight repertoire of the everyday cook, but right now you seldom find them there. Chinese cooking is often considered adventurous, ambitious, possibly admirable, but most of all, daunting and hard. Many a good cook has taken it up and gotten into it, but eventually the wok ends up in the garage and the dozen bottles of sauces skulk in the back of the fridge.

Quick & Easy Chinese is about cooking delicious Chinese dishes using ingredients you can easily find, tools you probably have, and the kind of time you can reasonably spare to make dinner at home. China being a rather large country with an abundance of people, climates, cultures, and cuisines, it makes sense, to me, to start small, with a reasonable, noble goal. The goal of this book is to share the everyday ways that I cook wonderful Chinese food at home for my family and friends, even on a busy day.

Bringing Chinese cooking home makes sense today. Access to traditional ingredients has never been better, with once-exotic sauces and condiments, fresh and dried noodles, and an abundance of gorgeous and good-for-you vegetables easily found around the country. Traditional cooking equipment is widely available, not that home cooks need anything fancy to cook everyday Chinese food. Stir-frying works beautifully in a large, deep skillet, and a good chef's knife does the chopping if a cleaver isn't among the *batterie de cuisine.*

To bring Chinese cooking home, it makes sense to focus on China's home cooking, the way literally millions of Chinese people cook in ordinary or even modest kitchens, every single day. Hong Kong seafood is fabulous, hand-tossed noodles are astounding, and dim sum parlors are a hoot, but none of these Chinese culinary experiences have much to do with a family cooking and eating dishes to go with rice. Starting with home cooking, I've worked out versions of traditional dishes that are simple, straightforward, and accessible to everyday cooks in the West, because that is exactly what they are within Chinese cuisine.

Here you will find recipes for Chinese dishes that are delicious and doable. My choices reflect the breadth and complexity of Chinese cooking, with dishes from Chinese home kitchens in the city and in the countryside; from overseas Chinese communities in Asia and in the West; from Singapore, Hong Kong, and Taiwan; and from the Chinese American restaurant repertoire, which was my first introduction to this extraordinary cuisine.

Like the land from which it grew, Chinese cooking is a big, bold, complicated, endlessly varied, mysterious, intriguing, and fascinating subject, full of detail, contradictions, and lore. Chinese restaurant menus bulge with edible offerings, but not every beloved Chinese dish is in this book. There are two reasons for not including them all. First, I adore going out for Chinese food. I love the round tables, the energy, and the chance to share dishes rather than choosing one entrée during a restaurant meal. Second, many classic Chinese restaurant dishes are beyond the scope of most home cooks, even in China.

Sizzling rice soup, whole fish steamed or fried, Peking duck, and honey-coated apples are a few of the not-quick-and-not-easy dishes well worth the journey to a Chinese restaurant.

Going out for Chinese food puts me and my family in a boisterous room full of happy people, feasting on an abundance of tasty dishes. Chinese people consider eating out a basic component of culinary life. They love dining out in restaurants plain and fancy, and they delight in picking up food to go from street vendors and food stalls. But what Chinese people still do, every day, all around the world, is cook simple, wonderful Chinese food at home. So do I, and so can you.

My wish for you is that this book guide you toward putting delicious Chinese dishes on your table, for your own delight and for people you enjoy. I hope that you enjoy shopping for the ingredients, chopping them up, and catching the aroma of garlic and ginger as they sizzle in the pan, and that as you toss and season and ladle out these dishes, you cook up lots of good times with family and friends.

When teaching my students about Chinese cooking, the quintessential message I present is to focus not on the first word, Chinese, but on the second word, cooking. Certainly even a small aquaintance with Asian cuisines shows that there is a world of difference, but the basic aspects which matter in home cooking are universal kitchen truths, useful anytime and anyplace you cook.

The key to happiness and good results in most cuisines, but particularly Asian cooking, is good knife skills. Knowing how to hold and use a good knife is extremely helpful to you in the kitchen. While books can convey many culinary techniques, knife work calls for observation and practice and ideally instruction from a person who knows knives as the primary kitchen tool. Look for classes at cooking schools in your area, within culinary arts programs at professional culinary schools, or in culinary arts programs at community colleges and technical institutes. Or talk to chefs and cooks in restaurants where you enjoy eating and see if you can work out a trade (perhaps your famous chutney, spiced almonds, or pound cake in exchange for a session of instruction in knife skills).

Preparation is the central step in Chinese cooking. An emphasis on sauces and seasonings stirred together and added during cooking; fresh vegetables and fragrant ingredients chopped, sliced, and minced; organizing ingredients; and setting the stage are crucial to enjoying the process, much more so than in the West. Here we employ an oven in which heat does its slow steady work, and a stove with many burners. With our tradition of cooking vegetables in pots with water and minor seasoning, many cooking steps can take place in sequence in Western cuisines.

Think of a stew, for which you season and brown meat in a heavy casserole, and then add onions, garlic, and a little wine and stock. Let it simmer awhile as you chop and add potatoes, mushrooms, and carrots, tossing in some thyme, and perhaps stirring in a roux at the end. Your process and pace differ considerably, as do the resulting dishes.

Within Chinese cuisine, the actual cooking time for many dishes, even soups, is measured in minutes, with a few or many small steps having been taken to set the stage. Often the preparation can be done ahead, or in stages. If you have someone helping you with these preparations, it creates pleasure while speeding things up a bit, though you can create these dishes without assistance, quickly and easily.

If you're planning a special Chinese meal, make yourself the executive chef. Think through what needs doing and when, and consider what you enjoy most. Then recruit a helper or two if you can, and delegate a few tasks to them. For the benefit of enjoying your cooking, you will probably find willing workers who take direction well, in anticipation of enjoying the result.

But remember that this is the quick and easy edition, in which laborious banquet menus are omitted and speedy and sensational weeknight dishes are the way to go. Even if you are on your own, a recipe like **Everyday Green Beans** (page 119) and a platter of **Ham-and-Egg Fried Rice** (page 134) can be on your table with a few minutes of preparation and a quick turn at the stove.

For equipment, keep it simple. A wok is designed for stir-frying and can be adapted for steaming and stews as well; but a large, deep skillet and the usual saucepans of a Western kitchen are all you need for cooking the dishes in this book. Spatulas that turn burgers and pancakes will work fine for scooping and tossing lo mein noodles, and a pair of spring-loaded V-shaped metal tongs makes a fantastic stand-in for cooking chopsticks and for working with any kind of noodles or pasta.

For insight into the world of wok-cooking, both in terms of traditional culture and of getting a tasty dinner on the table, spend time with *The Breath of a Wok*, by Grace Young (see page 182). Even if you don't own a wok or plan to buy one, Ms. Young opens a window into the Chinese kitchen, and you will enjoy the view.

GLOSSARY OF CHINESE INGREDIENTS

ASIAN SESAME OIL

This is made from white sesame seeds that are toasted to an aromatic, golden-brown state and then ground to extract their oil. Treasured predominantly for seasoning rather than cooking, this tea-colored oil comes in small glass bottles and is used throughout Asia, a teaspoon or two at a time, to flavor soups, dressings, stir-fried dishes, dipping sauces, and more. I consider it an essential item in my pantry, along with soy sauce; it provides extraordinary and delicious flavor and aroma in the simplest way, a drop or a dollop at a time.

ASIAN SESAME PASTE

Like tahini, Chinese-style sesame paste is made by grinding up white sesame seeds, but in this case the seeds are toasted first to develop a nutty flavor and handsome café au lait color. Typical brands come in 7-ounce jars, possibly labeled "sesame sauce" rather than "sesame paste." Expect the paste to be very thick, and possibly with a thin layer of oil on top. Use a fork to carefully mix the oil back in a little, but don't worry; mixed or not, it will deliver marvelous flavor. Peanut butter makes a very good substitute, with freshly ground unsweetened types providing the closest match. Asian sesame paste keeps for about 2 months on the counter and a little longer if refrigerated.

CHENKIANG RICE VINEGAR

Made from sticky rice and salt, this robust Chinese vinegar provides a handsome, deep-brown color as well as rich, complex flavor to Chinese sauces, pickles, stir-fries, and dipping sauces. You can substitute red wine vinegar, apple cider vinegar, or even balsamic vinegar with good results.

CHILI OIL

A fiery essence of dried red chili flakes cooked in very hot oil, this condiment is widely available in Asian markets, and also easy to make at home (page 175). You can use the oil only, or a mixture of oil and chilis and seeds right from the jar, in dipping sauces, marainades, and any recipe calling for chili sauce or hot sauce.

CHILI-GARLIC SAUCE

This chili sauce is made from fresh hot red chiles mashed up with garlic, vinegar, and salt,

creating a thick, tomato-red puree, fiery and delicious with visible seeds. Asian markets have it, but you can also find it in many supermarkets, sold in small plastic jars with parrot-green lids and a rooster on the label.

CHINESE-STYLE BLACK BEANS

See *Fermented Black Beans*.

CILANTRO

Soft, lacy leaves of cilantro provide bright flavor and aroma to many Chinese dishes, and are enjoyed as a beautiful jolt of color to finished dishes as well. You'll find it in produce sections around the country, sometimes labeled Chinese parsley, or coriander, since it is the leafy green plant grown from coriander seeds. I keep a bunch on hand and use it often. I like to put its roots in a jar of water and keep it out on my kitchen counter, along with the ginger, garlic, onions, and dried chilies, so that I can use it easily. If you wanted to store it for a few days, put roots or ends in a jar of water, cover the leaves loosely with a plastic or paper bag from the produce section, and store in the refrigerator for up to 4 days.

DARK SOY SAUCE

This is soy sauce with heft and hue, more of an increase in color and richness than in the salty character for which regular soy sauce is valued. You use this by the teaspoons, and a tiny splash turns a stir-fried dish a magnificent caramel-colored hue, while harmonizing with other flavors in the dish. I list it as optional in many dishes, since its role is often (though not always) to be colorful rather than to mediate the flavor. But if you can buy a bottle or two from an Asian source (see page 186) and keep it on hand, you will get lots of service and pleasure from it.

DRIED RED CHILI PEPPER FLAKES

Keep these on hand for scattering into stir-fries when you want a little heat, or a lot. The texture adds beauty as well as a complex heat, better to me than plain old finely ground chilies or cayenne. You can also make chili oil using these chili flakes (page 175), but treat yourself to a fresh supply if yours has been on the shelf for longer than a few months. It stays hot but loses some character, so I like to toss it into the compost and start a new culinary fire with a fresh supply now and then.

BLACK BEANS

Made from small black soy beans that are salt-preserved and fermented to develop a deep, tangy flavor, Chinese-style black beans deliver fantastic flavor to many Asian dishes. Especially popular with clams, whole fish, and other seafood, black beans tend to be chopped up or mashed with garlic and ginger before use, and then added to dishes which are stir-fried or steamed. You'll find them in cellophane or plastic bags, or in cylindrical cardboard containers. They should be soft to the touch. Transferred to a glass jar and kept away from heat and air, they should last indefinitely at room temperature.

FIVE-SPICE POWDER

This spice mixture is a signature seasoning of the Western region of China, and is valued as a complement to braised dishes, stir-fries, and grilled food. Made from star anise, cinnamon, Szechuan peppercorns, fennel, and cloves, five-spice powder infuses its sweet-smoky flavor into marinades for poultry and meat, which are then roasted to an aromatic and flavorful perfection.

GARLIC

Keeping fresh garlic handy gives you extraordinary flavor for simple dishes. Many supermarkets carry peeled whole cloves in jars, which make chopped garlic a very quickly produced ingredient for busy cooks. You can also use a Chinese cleaver or a chef's knife to get into garlic cloves quickly, placing a clove on your cutting board, placing the flat blade of either knife on the clove with the sharp edge away from you, and giving the flat side of the knife a good thump with your fist. The paper will pop open and easily fall away, and the clove will be split open and easy to chop.

GINGER

Get to know fresh ginger if you don't already consider it part of your elementary kitchen essentials. Sliced in thin coins, cut into shreds or slivers, or finely chopped for adding to stir-fries and stews, fresh ginger is an incomparable powerhouse of brilliant, cool, and astringent flavor that makes an extraordinary difference in simple dishes with very little work. I use it constantly in all kinds of dishes, and keep it out on the counter with the garlic, dried chiles, and onions so that I won't forget I have it on hand. I buy it often in smaller amounts since I can always find it at my supermarket, where it is stored at room temperature. To keep it long term, you could trim away any soft or tired-looking portions, wrap it loosely in paper towels, and put it in a paper bag or open plastic bag in the crisper.

GREEN ONIONS

Keeping a bunch or two of these familiar produce items makes great sense when you're cooking Chinese and Asian food. You will use them often, for their color, flavor, and beauty; it's an item to pick up often at the store.

HOISIN SAUCE

As thick as apple butter and endowed with a deep, plush sweetness, hoisin sauce is an adored member of the family of bean sauces, which have been valued in Chinese cuisine since ancient times. Made from fermented soybeans ground to thick paste with garlic, sugar, and an array of spices, hoisin sauce serves many kitchen purposes, adding its color and sweet-salty flavor notes to marinades, glazes, dipping sauces, stir-fries, and barbecue sauces for roasted and grilled poultry and meat. Keep it in its jar in the refrigerator for about 6 months.

KETCAP MANIS

Dark soy sauce or dark sweet soy sauce. Fortified with a deep sweetness by the addition of molasses, this mahogany-colored essence is used extensively in the cooking of Malaysia, Singapore, and Indonesia. Use it in place of dark soy sauce in recipes. A treasure any time you want to add deep, rich color to a dish; start with ½ teaspoon, as even a little bestows gorgeous brown hues to any food. Look for it in tall bottles in Asian markets. It keeps indefinitely at room temperature.

OYSTER SAUCE

This lustrous dark-brown essence is a salty signature of Cantonese cooking, though it is known and enjoyed throughout the cuisines of China. Made from an extract of dried, salted oysters, it is enjoyed directly as a condiment and sauce as well as in combination with other ingredients for cooking. Unlike soy sauce and many other Asian seasonings, oyster sauce is perishable and should be kept in the refrigerator.

ROCK SUGAR

This looks like a rough gemstone right out of the quarry, with its translucent amber color and hard yet crumbly texture. It's actually much softer than it looks; you can break or cut it fairly easily, though it seems at first to be indeed a kind of rock. It is cane sugar and honey combined in a crystallized form, and is also called yellow sugar and yellow lump sugar in various translations. Especially cherished in northern Chinese cooking, it contributes an incomparable lush texture and gloss to red-cooked dishes, which are meat, poultry, or fish braised in dark soy sauce, rock sugar, and rice wine. Don't worry about smashing it down to a state you can measure in a tablespoon—just break it up into reasonable chunks and eyeball it. A little extra will never be a bad thing, and I consider a walnut-sized lump to be pretty close to a tablespoon. Buy a box, since the packaging is charming and low-tech, the cost is minimal, the look is fascinating, and the flavor

is divine, whether you dissolve it in your tea, lemonade, or red-cooked chicken braise.

SESAME OIL

See *Asian sesame oil*.

SHAOXING RICE WINE

Made from sticky rice and named after the town where it is traditionally made, Shaoxing rice wine is an amber-colored fortified wine, widely available in Asian markets. One standard brand is sold in brown bottles with a big red label. If you can visit a Chinese-owned liquor store, ask about various versions of the spirit; you could use any of them in your cooking.

SHERRY

Dry sherry, such as amontillado, is a very good substitute for Shaoxing rice wine, a traditional component of countless Chinese dishes. You could also use white wine or chicken stock if neither sherry nor Shaoxing rice wine is available or if you need a substitute.

SOY SAUCE

If you've kept a modest little bottle of soy sauce in the cabinet or on the fridge door, it's time to move up. You will use soy sauce often in these recipes, so consider the biggest bottle you can find at the supermarket lest you run out at suppertime. Soy sauce is an ancient seasoning made from salted, fermented soybeans. It adds color and depth as well as its specific salty flavor to an array of dishes in this book, and belongs among your everyday seasonings if it's not already there.

SZECHUAN PEPPERCORNS

The powerfully flavorful berries of the prickly ash tree, Szechuan peppercorns provide a zingy, intense and pungent flavor to numerous dishes originating in the Western Chinese provinces of Szechuan and Hunan. As prickly ash berries ripen to a rusty red, they split open and curl back like petals, exposing an ivory interior with tiny dark seeds. Adored for their oddly wonderful and numbing sensation of heat and flavor, Szechuan peppercorns pair wonderfully with rich and luscious dishes made with pork and duck. Usually toasted before being ground to a coarse or fine powder, this distinctive spice is mixed with warm salt to make a tasty dip for grilled meat.

SZECHUAN PRESERVED VEGETABLES

This salty-hot pickle is fermented with chilies, garlic, and salt in great tubs, and then preserved in brine. Rinsed before use, it is chopped up and added to stir-fries, soups, and braised dishes for its contribution of tangy crunch and intense salty heat. Sold in plastic packets, it should be transferred to a jar and stored in the refrigerator for up to 2 months.

appetizers & snacks

Whether you're on a Beijing side street, a Shanghai street corner, or a winding Chinatown sidewalk in New York City, you will find evidence aplenty that the Chinese love food. Watch people cooking, eating, buying, and selling food, and carrying it along to share with someone else, anytime and anywhere Chinese people are awake.

The variety and range of things to eat on short notice is a testament to the dedication Chinese people have to eating with pleasure, and this kind of food translates wonderfully into starters you can make for any gathering. Street food is a natural for this category, since it tends to be simple-to-eat, stand-alone fare, rather than a component of a rice-centered meal. Favorite appetizers on the menu of Chinese restaurants in the West are often versions of street-food classics, from spring rolls and spareribs to dumplings and deep-fried treats.

Many street-food specialties take time and years of expertise to master, but a number of these small dishes translate wonderfully to a home kitchen and make a delicious addition to your repertoire of starters. In this chapter you'll find Honey-Ginger Spareribs (page 26), Soy Sauce Chicken Wings (page 27), Cold Sesame Noodles (page 31), and Hoisin Shrimp in Lettuce Cups (page 21), each of which is simple enough for your standard party menus. Pot Sticker Dumplings with Ginger-Soy Dipping Sauce (page 23) and Green Onion Pancakes (page 29) can be wrapped up and rolled out ahead of time, and then quickly cooked and served when you are ready to enjoy them.

When Chinese hosts present an appetizer course, it often begins a multicourse banquet and is waiting on the banquet table when the guests arrive. Even if restaurant chefs are doing the cooking, the focus is on a gracious welcome for guests and minimum attention from the cooks, who have, perhaps literally, bigger fish to fry. Traditional starters include cold cuts, a pedestrian name in the West but a Chinese category of great bites including thinly sliced ham, Char Shiu Pork (page 98), abalone, and nuts, including freshly fried cashews or peanuts, or Candied Walnuts (page 166).

To follow this wise tradition, consider designing your party menu in the same spirit, weaving in recipes from your standard starter repertoire with a dish or two from this chapter. For cold cuts, arrange smoked salmon, prosciutto, and thinly sliced salami or summer sausage on handsome plates. For nuts, set out ready-to-eat pistachios and roasted, salted cashews, along with smoked almonds or honey-roasted peanuts. Add a pile of boiled, chilled shrimp with Ginger-Soy Dipping Sauce (page 171) and spicy cocktail sauce, and an item or two from this chapter, and you're done. You may enjoy your small plates theme so much that you add a few more and call it a meal, with lots of room and time for guests to sample and savor along with you.

HOISIN SHRIMP in lettuce cups

This dish pairs the delicate, sweet notes of shrimp with the earthy sweetness of hoisin sauce, with delicious results. Don't let the long ingredients list deter you. You simply stir the seasonings into a sauce that is tossed with the shrimp and zucchini at the end of cooking. Serve this with lettuce cups on the side or spoon it into lettuce cups for a cool and flavorful starter, to be eaten out of hand.

¾ pound medium shrimp, peeled and deveined

1 small zucchini

1 tablespoon hoisin sauce

1 tablespoon dry sherry or Shaoxing rice wine

1 tablespoon chicken broth or water

2 teaspoons soy sauce

½ teaspoon sugar

½ teaspoon salt

2 tablespoons vegetable oil

1 tablespoon chopped garlic

2 teaspoons chopped fresh ginger

continued on next page

SERVES **4**

✳ Chop the shrimp into small chunks, about ¼ inch in diameter (see Note). Trim the zucchini and chop it into ¼-inch chunks too. In a small bowl, combine the hoisin sauce, sherry, chicken broth, soy sauce, sugar, and salt, and stir to mix well.

✳ Heat a wok or a large, deep skillet over high heat until a drop of water sizzles at once. Add the vegetable oil and swirl to coat the pan evenly. Scatter in the garlic and ginger, and toss them well. When they are fragrant, about 15 seconds, add the shrimp and cook, tossing often, until pink on the outside, about 1 minute.

✳ Add the zucchini and toss well. Cook, tossing often, until the zucchini are bright green and tender, and the shrimp are cooked through. Add the hoisin sauce mixture, pouring it in around the sides of the pan, and then toss to season everything evenly. Add the sesame oil, cilantro, and green onion, and toss to combine well.

➤ ➤ ➤

½ teaspoon Asian sesame oil

2 tablespoons finely chopped
cilantro leaves

2 tablespoons finely chopped
green onion

About 20 cup-shaped lettuce leaves,
such as Bibb, Boston, or iceberg

NOTE *To chop the shrimp, cut the tail por-*
tion into two or three pieces. Then halve
the thick upper portion lengthwise and cut
it crosswise into two or three sections.

✶ Transfer to a serving platter, with lettuce leaves on the side, and invite guests to spoon shrimp into lettuce leaves to make small wraps. Or, spoon shrimp into lettuce cups and arrange the filled lettuce leaves on a serving platter.

POT STICKER DUMPLINGS with ginger-soy dipping sauce

These delectable dumplings are first fried, then steamed, endowing them with a fabulous dual texture. Smooth, luscious noodlelike wrapping and tender, meaty filling complement the handsomely browned bottom crust. Round *gyoza* wrappers, available in Asian markets and many supermarkets, are ideal here; but won ton wrappers work wonderfully if you trim off the four corners before wrapping your dumplings. Though these treats are quick and easy to cook, the mixing and wrapping steps take a little time. Plan to make them a day ahead and refrigerate or freeze them. Or follow Chinese tradition and invite guests to come fill, shape, and cook dumplings along with you, making the preparation and cooking part of the party.

1 pound ground pork or ground beef

¼ cup thinly sliced green onion

1 tablespoon soy sauce

1 tablespoon Asian sesame oil

2 teaspoons finely chopped fresh ginger

1 teaspoon salt

½ teaspoon sugar

¼ cup frozen chopped spinach, thawed
(see Note)

continued on next page

MAKES ABOUT **36** POT STICKERS

✳ In a large bowl, combine the pork, green onion, soy sauce, sesame oil, ginger, salt, and sugar. Squeeze the spinach with your hands or press it into a strainer, extracting most of the water. Add the spinach to the bowl and use a large spoon or your hands to mix everything together until all the seasonings are incorporated and the spinach and green onion are evenly mixed in.

✳ To fold the dumplings, set up a work space with a dry cutting board, a small bowl of water for sealing the dumplings, the stack of won ton wrappers, and the pork mixture.

✳ To shape a potsticker dumpling, place a wrapper on the cutting board. Scoop up a generous tablespoon of pork filling and place it in the center of the wrapper. Dip your index finger into the bowl of water, then lightly moisten the outside edge of the wrapper. Fold it in half, enclosing the filling

36 won ton wrappers or round *gyoza* wrappers (10-oz to 12-oz packages have about 50 wrappers each)

2 tablespoons vegetable oil

½ cup water

Ginger-Soy Dipping Sauce (page 171)

🍡🍡🍡

NOTE *You could also use blanched fresh spinach: drop about 4 cups loosely packed spinach into a small pot of boiling water, let cook 1 minute, drain well, squeeze gently but firmly to extract water, coarsely chop, and measure out ¼ cup. To use napa cabbage or regular cabbage, you could chop it finely and use it raw or blanched.*

🍡🍡🍡

and pinching the top edges to make a tight seal. Try to squeeze out any air bubbles that may form. Create 3 small pleats on one side of the seal, folding toward the center and pressing to seal it well. Form 3 small pleats on the other side and press the entire sealed edge. Press the sealed edge down lightly to plump up the dumpling and make it stand up straight.

✳ Continue folding dumplings in this way, one at a time, or setting up 3 or 4 wrappers at a time for an assembly line. Place the folded dumplings in rows on a dry platter so that they don't touch each other.

✳ To cook the potstickers, heat a 10-inch nonstick skillet over medium-high heat and then add the vegetable oil and swirl to coat the pan. Carefully place about 12 potstickers in the pan, tucking them to form a circle in one direction; squeeze a few into the center if you can. (Packing them tightly is fine.) Place a serving platter by the stove to hold the cooked dumplings.

✳ Let them cook undisturbed for 1 to 2 minutes, until the bottoms of the dumplings are a pale golden brown. Holding the skillet's lid in one hand, add ½ cup water around the sides of the pan and then cover quickly. Let potstickers cook for 8 minutes, and then uncover the pan.

✳ Continue cooking 1 to 2 minutes more, shaking the pan gently and using a spatula to discourage the pot stickers from sticking too much. When the water has evaporated and the dumplings are a handsome crispy brown, turn them out bottom side up onto a serving platter. Serve hot or warm, accompanied by Ginger-Soy Dipping Sauce.

HONEY-GINGER SPARERIBS

You can use regular or baby back ribs in this recipe, cutting the rack into individual ribs before marinating them so that they cook and brown quickly and evenly. Call ahead to make sure that the butcher at your supermarket meat counter will have what you need. Let the ribs marinate in the sauce for 30 minutes, or cover and refrigerate them to marinate as long as overnight.

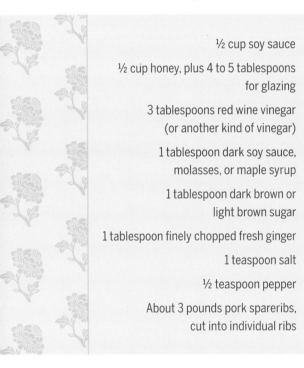

½ cup soy sauce

½ cup honey, plus 4 to 5 tablespoons for glazing

3 tablespoons red wine vinegar (or another kind of vinegar)

1 tablespoon dark soy sauce, molasses, or maple syrup

1 tablespoon dark brown or light brown sugar

1 tablespoon finely chopped fresh ginger

1 teaspoon salt

½ teaspoon pepper

About 3 pounds pork spareribs, cut into individual ribs

MAKES ABOUT **24** RIBS, ENOUGH FOR **4** PEOPLE

❋ In a large bowl, combine the soy sauce, ½ cup honey, vinegar, dark soy sauce, brown sugar, ginger, salt, and pepper. Stir well, until the sugar dissolves and the soy sauce and honey combine to make a smooth marinade.

❋ Add the spareribs to the bowl and turn to coat them evenly with the marinade. Set aside for 30 minutes, or cover and refrigerate for up to 1 day. Turn them once or twice to season them evenly.

❋ To cook, heat the oven to 350°F. Line a large rimmed baking sheet or roasting pan completely with aluminum foil, to keep cleanup easy. Arrange the seasoned ribs on the foil-lined pan individually, spaced a few inches apart to help them brown evenly. Place the pan in the oven and roast for 20 minutes.

❋ Remove the pan, turn the ribs over, and then continue roasting for 15 to 20 minutes more, until the ribs are evenly browned and cooked through. Increase the heat to 400°F and cook another 5 minutes.

❋ Remove the ribs from the oven and push them together into a low pile in the center of the pan. Drizzle the reserved honey over the ribs, and then turn and tumble the ribs a few times, to coat them evenly with the honey. Transfer to a serving platter and serve hot, warm, or at room temperature.

SOY SAUCE CHICKEN WINGS

This simple recipe gives you a delicious-looking pile of wings to serve warm or at room temperature. Perfect for a picnic or potluck, they can be made ahead and reheated gently, or chilled and brought to room temperature on the way to an event. I remove the wing tip and either discard it or save it in the freezer for stock, but it's fine to leave wings whole. You can use trimmed chicken wings or "drummettes," the first portion or drumstick, or "Buffalo wings," the first two joints divided with the third joint removed. Whatever form you use, choose a saucepan that keeps the wings covered with sauce as they cook, rather than spread out in a single layer.

1½ cups soy sauce

¾ cup water

¼ cup dark or light brown sugar

3 tablespoons molasses or honey

1 teaspoon salt

¼ cup very coarsely chopped fresh ginger

8 slices fresh ginger

3 green onions, cut crosswise into 2-inch lengths

1½ pounds chicken wings

SERVES **4** TO **6**

✳ In a large saucepan, combine the soy sauce, water, brown sugar, molasses, salt, ginger, and green onions. Stir to dissolve the sugar and salt, and then bring to a boil over medium-high heat.

✳ Carefully add the chicken wings to the pot. They should crowd the pot and be almost covered with the sauce. Let the sauce return to a boil, and then adjust the heat to maintain a lively, visible simmer.

✳ Let the chicken wings boil gently for 12 minutes, stirring once or twice to make sure that the wings cook and color evenly. Remove from the heat and leave the wings in the sauce to finish cooking and deepen in color, about 30 minutes.

✳ Transfer the wings to a serving platter. Remove and discard the ginger slices and green onions. Serve hot, warm, or at room temperature.

GREEN ONION PANCAKES

These fabulous street-food flatbreads show up in night markets and in street-food centers all over Asia. On our annual visits to Taiwan, my family and I eagerly seek out the couple who serve them up from a simple stall by the Taipei subway stop near the Sun Yat-Sen Memorial. Theirs are incomparably delicious, but these are very tasty, lovely to look at, and amazingly simple to make. Plan to roll and cook the pancakes one at a time while you're learning, and then speed up once you've got it down.

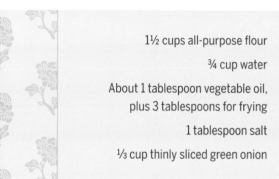

1½ cups all-purpose flour

¾ cup water

About 1 tablespoon vegetable oil, plus 3 tablespoons for frying

1 tablespoon salt

⅓ cup thinly sliced green onion

MAKES **3** PANCAKES; SERVES **4** TO **6**

✳ In a medium bowl, combine the flour and water. Stir well to mix it up and turn it into a soft dough.

✳ Lightly flour a work surface and your hands, and then scrape the dough out onto the floured work surface. Knead the dough for 5 minutes, turning and pressing to form it into a soft, smooth dough. Cover the dough with the bowl for a five-minute rest.

✳ Divide the dough into 3 portions, cutting it apart with a butter knife or pastry scraper. Leaving the other two portions covered while you work, place one portion on the floured work surface, and roll it out into a big, round pancake, 6 to 8 inches in diameter.

✳ Use about 1 teaspoon of the oil to lightly and evenly coat the surface of the pancake. Sprinkle it with 1 teaspoon of the salt, and then scatter about ⅓ of the green onion over the pancake.

✳ Starting with the far edge and pulling it toward you, carefully roll up the pancake into a plump log. The soft dough will need a little coaxing, and it won't be perfectly even, but that is just fine.

✳ Shape the log into a fat spiral, turning the right end toward you to make the center and curving the remaining log around it. Tuck the loose end under and gently but firmly press to flatten it into a big, thick cake. Using your rolling pin, roll it gently into a 7-inch pancake. The green onion will tear the dough and poke out here and there, but that's not a problem.

✳ To cook, heat a heavy, medium skillet over medium-high heat until hot. Add about 2 teaspoons of the oil and turn to coat the bottom of the pan evenly. When a pinch of dough and a bit of green onion sizzle at once, place the pancake in the hot pan and cook until handsomely browned and fairly evenly cooked on one side, 2 to 3 minutes.

✳ Turn and cook the other side for about 1 minute, until it is nicely browned and the bread is cooked through. Use the remaining dough to roll out, season, shape, and cook two more pancakes. Use additional oil as needed. Cut into quarters, and serve hot or warm.

COLD SESAME NOODLES

I adore sesame noodles and marvel at how simple it is to make this satisfying and unusual dish. Since they taste wonderful warm, at room temperature, or cold, they make delightful party or picnic fare. Asian noodles are traditional, but linguine or spaghetti cooked al dente work fine, and peanut butter makes a tasty substitute for toasted sesame paste. I like to stir the sauce together first and then cook the noodles just before serving time. I often add chopped green onion or cilantro along with the cucumber for extra flavor and color.

FOR THE SESAME SAUCE

3 tablespoons Asian sesame paste or peanut butter

2 tablespoons soy sauce

2 tablespoons hot water

2 teaspoons red wine vinegar or cider vinegar

2 teaspooons sugar

1 teaspoon dark soy sauce (optional)

1 teaspoon Asian sesame oil

1 teaspoon **Hot Chili Oil** (page 175) or another hot sauce or chili paste

½ teaspoon salt

continued on next page

✳ To make the sesame sauce: In a medium bowl large enough to toss the noodles with the sauce, combine the sesame paste, soy sauce, water, vinegar, sugar, dark soy sauce, if using, sesame oil, chili oil, and salt. Stir to combine everything into a smooth, thick sauce.

✳ To make the noodles: Bring a large pot of water to a rolling boil over high heat. Drop in the egg noodles and cook until tender but still firm, stirring now and again to separate them and help them cook evenly, about 2 minutes.

✳ When the noodles are tender but still firm, drain well and place them in the bowl over the sauce. Toss well to coat the strands evenly. Add a little more hot water if needed to soften the noodles and spread out the sauce.

➤ ➤ ➤

SERVES **4**

FOR THE NOODLES

8 ounces fresh Chinese-style egg noodles (or linguini or spaghetti, if necessary)

⅓ cup thinly sliced green onion

¼ cup finely chopped Szechuan preserved vegetable (optional)

3 tablespoons chopped roasted, salted peanuts

1 cup cucumber slices (¼ inch thick)

✳ Add the green onion, Szechuan preserved vegetable, peanuts, and cucumber, and toss one last time to mix everything well. Transfer to a serving plate and serve warm, at room temperature, or cold.

TEA EGGS

Eggs mean breakfast in Western cuisines, but in Asia they mean hearty, pleasing fare at almost any meal. Rich and satisfying with their smooth texture and sweet hints of star anise and soy flavors, they shine as snacks, starters, or picnic fare, as well as a handsome component of any rice-centered meal. We love them with thick-sliced ripe tomatoes with fresh basil, Bok Choy Stir-Fried with Garlic (page 120), and Cold Sesame Noodles (page 31) for a tasty vegetarian supper.

8 eggs

4 cups water

2 teabags of any black tea, such as orange pekoe

1 tablespoon dark soy sauce or molasses, or 3 tablespoons soy sauce

1½ teaspoons salt

1 piece star anise, or 1 tablespoon five-spice powder (see page 14)

SERVES **4**

❧❧❧

NOTE *Tea eggs taste great and look wonderful to me, no matter how the tea and dark soy sauce infusion displays itself. Wherever the eggshell cracks completely, lots of color seeps in, and it's likely that you'll have some larger cracks in the process of rolling the eggs to make tiny cracks. Enjoy the surprise of peeling your tea eggs, and make them often so you develop your skills.*

❧❧❧

✳ Place the eggs in a medium saucepan and add enough cold water to cover them. Bring to a gentle boil over medium heat and cook 5 minutes. Drain, rinse well with cold water, and let stand in cold water for 5 minutes.

✳ Drain eggs well and set them out on a plate. Holding one egg in your hand, tap it gently but firmly with the back of a spoon to create tiny cracks all over its shell. Turn it in your hand as you work. You can also place it on the countertop and roll it gently to crack the shell. Repeat with remaining eggs, and then set them aside while you prepare their tea infusion.

✳ Bring the 4 cups water to a rolling boil over high heat in the same saucepan. Add the teabags, dark soy sauce, salt, and star anise, and stir well. When the tea infusion comes to a rolling boil, reduce the heat to medium and use a large spoon to carefully lower the cracked eggs into the pot. Add water if needed so that the infusion covers the eggs completely. Adjust the heat to maintain a gentle but lively simmer, visible on the surface, and let the eggs cook for 30 minutes.

✳ Remove from the heat and let stand for 1 hour. (You could also refrigerate overnight for deeper color and flavor.) Remove from the broth and carefully peel each egg to remove the cracked shell. Serve whole or halved and placed cut side down, warm or at room temperature.

soups

Chinese meals count on soup as a component, almost as a beverage or touchstone in a menu of varied flavors designed to go with an abundance of rice. Many soups are quite simple, consisting of chicken stock with small pieces of meat or seafood, some leafy greens or shreds of vegetable, and an accent of sesame oil, green onions, or cilantro to brighten the bowl.

Most are made well within an hour of serving time, unlike the Western tradition of simmering a soup on the back of the stove for hours, and making it thick with vegetables and meat. Chowders, minestrone, and vegetable-beef soup are examples of this soup-as-the-star tradition, and while we love them, they tend to be major cooking projects. In contrast, these Chinese-style soups are ones to stir together while the rice steams or the pasta pot boils, and to enjoy along with a stir-fried dish, rotisserie chicken, an herb-laced omelet, or grilled fish. Egg Flower Soup (page 38) and Meatball Soup with Spinach (page 37) are excellent examples of this busy-day genre of soup.

Creamy Corn Soup with Ham (page 43) and Hot and Sour Soup (page 44) are each a little more involved, but either could serve as the main course along with wonderful bread and butter and a big green salad or steamed broccoli. Won Ton Soup (page 40) is quick and easy once the won tons are shaped, but you will want to plan a won ton–making session on a Saturday morning or on a day when you're making dinner without watching the clock. Extra hands make it fast and fun, and for a meal of won tons or a batch to take home, you will most likely find many potential helpers eager to sign up. It takes time to get won tons lined up on a tray, but once you're done, it is a feast in a bowl, and keeping a batch in the freezer, uncooked, is insurance for the day when you long for a fabulous Chinese feast in a very short time.

MEATBALL SOUP with spinach

We love this hearty soup with rice and a simple vegetable stir-fry like Everyday Green Beans (page 119) or Broccoli with Garlic and Ginger (page 127). You can roll the meat into little balls or just add it in free-form pinches to the boiling soup. Add carrot shreds, tofu chunks, or sliced mushrooms right after the meat if you want a more complex dish without much more effort.

1 small bundle bean thread noodles (about 2 ounces)

¼ pound ground pork

2 teaspoons soy sauce

1 teaspoon finely chopped garlic

½ teaspooon salt

4 cups chicken stock

2 cups fresh baby spinach leaves, or large leaves torn into 2-inch pieces

3 tablespoons thinly sliced green onion

Asian sesame oil (optional)

SERVES **4**

✳ Soften the bean thread noodles by placing them in a medium bowl with warm water to cover for 15 minutes. When they are flexible and white, cut them into 3-inch lengths and set aside.

✳ Combine the pork with the soy sauce, garlic, and salt and mix together to season the meat evenly. Roll the mixture into small meatballs, about 1 inch in diameter, or use a spoon to scoop it into small, free-form meatballs.

✳ In a medium saucepan, bring the chicken stock to a rolling boil over high heat. Drop the meatballs into the boiling soup, a few at a time, and stir to keep them from sticking together. When all the meatballs are in the soup, adjust the heat to maintain a gentle boil and cook for 3 minutes. Skim off and discard any foam that forms on the soup, and stir now and then.

✳ Add the noodles and stir well, cooking until they become clear and soft, about 1 minute more. Add the spinach and green onion and remove from the heat. Serve hot, adding a few drops of sesame oil, if using, to the soup just before serving.

EGG FLOWER SOUP

Often listed as Egg Drop Soup in Chinese restaurants, this dish's poetic name of Egg Flower Soup celebrates the way eggs "blossom" as they are stirred gently into simmering stock. If you use canned broth or frozen chicken stock, this soup makes a perfect busy-night dish. If you make chicken stock, this dish showcases its deep flavor with delicious simplicity. Either way, Egg Flower Soup rounds out any rice-centered meal, and it can be served in big bowls over rice as a one-dish dinner. Plan to stir in the eggs just before serving for the most wonderful texture and beauty.

4 cups chicken stock

2 cups baby spinach leaves (optional)

½ teaspoon Asian sesame oil

½ teaspoon salt

2 well-beaten eggs

3 tablespoons thinly sliced green onion

SERVES **4**

✳ In a medium saucepan, bring the chicken stock to a rolling boil over medium-high heat. Stir in the spinach leaves, if using, sesame oil, and salt, allowing the spinach to wilt into the soup.

✳ Stir well until the chicken broth is swirling in circles. Carefully and slowly pour the beaten eggs onto the surface of the soup, continuing to stir gently and encouraging them to flow out into leafy petals and ribbons.

✳ Sprinkle the green onion onto the soup and serve hot.

WON TON SOUP

From my first tiny bowl of won ton soup at Wong's Chinese Restaurant in my North Carolina hometown, I have loved this soup. I've since enjoyed it in New York City and San Francisco, as well as in Hong Kong, Bangkok, and Taipei. The fact that every little won ton needs filling, folding, and cooking means that this dish doesn't belong in the busy-weeknight category. But made in advance with only a few ingredients and simple steps, these dumplings are ready to boil and enjoy in soup or with a simple sauce, right from the freezer or fridge. Helpers recruited from among friends and family make this task a pleasure, and the reward of won ton soup will make them eager to sign up for future sessions. I love sprinkling a spoonful of Asian sesame oil onto my soup along with the green onion and cilantro leaves.

FOR THE WON TONS
¾ pound ground pork

2 tablespoons finely chopped green onion

1 tablespoon soy sauce

1 teaspoon Asian sesame oil

½ teaspoon salt

About 40 square won ton wrappers

12 cups water, plus 3 cups cold

SERVES **6** TO **8**

✳ To make the won tons: Combine the pork, green onion, soy sauce, sesame oil, and salt in a medium bowl. Stir to mix everything evenly.

✳ Prepare to fold the won tons by arranging the following on a table where you can sit and work: the package of won ton wrappers, measuring spoons, a small bowl of water to use when sealing the filled won tons, a cutting board or tray on which to lay out the wrappers as you fill them, and a platter or cookie sheet on which to place the filled won tons as you work.

✳ Place a wrapper before you, and put about 1 teaspoon of filling in the center of the wrapper. Moisten the edges of the wrapper with a little water and fold it into a triangle shape. Press the edges together to seal it well. Bring the two bottom corners of the triangle together, and seal them with a little water, making a plump little envelope with the top point free. Set aside and continue filling wrappers. You will have around 40 won tons.

FOR THE SOUP

6 cups chicken stock

2 cups fresh baby spinach leaves, or large spinach leaves torn into 2-inch pieces right before use

¼ cup chopped green onion

About ⅓ cup chopped fresh cilantro leaves

ᵔᵔᵔ

NOTE *You could also prepare individual bowls, noodle shop–style. Set out a bowl for each guest near the stove. Place hot won tons in each bowl, and add a few leaves of spinach. Ladle hot soup into each bowl, sprinkle with green onion and cilantro leaves, and serve hot.*

ᵔᵔᵔ

(To freeze them, place them on a platter which will fit in the freezer, at least 1 inch apart. When they are completely frozen, place them in a resealable plastic bag or airtight container and store for up to 1 month. Don't thaw them but allow an extra few minutes' cooking time.)

✳ To cook the won tons, bring 12 cups water to a rolling boil in a large pot over high heat. Have the 3 cups cold water handy, along with a 1-cup measure. Drop the won tons into the boiling water one by one, stirring now and then to keep them separate. As soon as the water returns to a boil, add 1 cup of the cold water to stop the boiling.

✳ When the water boils again, add another cup of cold water. When it boils a third time, add the last cup of water. When it boils again, scoop the wontons out gently and drain well. Transfer to a large serving bowl or tureen in which you will serve the soup, and cover it to keep them warm while you make the soup.

✳ To make the soup: In a small saucepan over medium heat, bring the chicken stock to a boil. Place the spinach leaves in the serving bowl over the won tons and carefully pour the hot chicken stock over them. Sprinkle the green onion and cilantro on top, and serve at once. Provide soup bowls with spoons for soup and chopsticks or forks for won tons. Serve 5 or 6 won tons into each guest's bowl along with some spinach, green onion, and cilantro, top off with chicken stock, and serve hot.

CREAMY CORN SOUP with ham

Keep creamed corn and chicken stock on your pantry shelf and you will be minutes away from an inviting bowl of this golden-colored and satisfying soup. Chinese restaurant versions tend to include cornstarch to thicken it, but I love its texture without that addition.

Two 14½-ounce cans creamed corn (about 3 cups)

2 cups chicken stock

2 tablespoons dry sherry, Shaoxing rice wine, or white wine

1 teaspoon salt

¼ cup chopped ham, cooked crabmeat, salmon, or shrimp

1 teaspoon Asian sesame oil

3 tablespoons finely chopped green onion

SERVES **4**

✳ In a medium saucepan, combine the creamed corn and chicken stock, and bring to a gentle boil. Stir in the sherry and salt, and then add the ham. Cook for 1 minute more, stirring once or twice, until the soup is steaming hot and everything is evenly combined.

✳ Remove from the heat and stir in the sesame oil and green onion. Serve hot or warm.

NOTE *For a thicker, restaurant-style soup, simply mix 2 teaspoons cornstarch with 2 tablespoons cold water, stirring to dissolve. Add to the bubbling hot soup just before serving, stirring well. Remove from the heat as soon as you see that the soup has thickened up nicely. Then add the ham, sesame oil, and green onion, and serve hot.*

HOT AND SOUR SOUP

Try a steaming bowl of this pungent soup the next time you need help warming up on a cold winter's night. Abundant with contrasts in texture and flavor, it holds a place of honor on Chinese restaurant menus in the West and is enjoyed throughout China, far from its northern home. The traditional recipe calls for cloud ears and lily buds, also called "golden needles," two dried ingredients that need soaking and trimming in advance. I love this soup with Pot Sticker Dumplings (page 23) and a big, cool green salad, or with steamed broccoli and a bowl of rice.

5 dried shiitake mushrooms,
fresh shiitake mushrooms,
or button mushrooms

2 tablespoons Chenkiang vinegar,
red wine vinegar, or cider vinegar

1 tablespoon soy sauce

1 teaspoon **Hot Chili Oil** (page 175),
chili-garlic sauce, or red pepper flakes

½ teaspoon salt

½ teaspoon freshly ground pepper

2 teaspoons cornstarch

2 tablespoons water

SERVES **4** TO **6**

✳ Cover the dried mushrooms with warm water and soak for 20 minutes, until they are softened. If using dried softened shiitakes or fresh shiitakes, remove the stems and cut the caps into long thin strips. If using another type of mushroom, cut lengthwise into thin slices or strips.

✳ In a medium bowl, combine the vinegar, soy sauce, chili oil, salt, and pepper, and stir to combine everything well. In a small bowl, combine the cornstarch and water and mix them well. Cut the pork crosswise into thin slices and then lengthwise into long, thin strips.

✳ Bring the chicken stock to a boil in a large saucepan over medium-high heat. Add the pork, mushrooms, carrots, bamboo shoots, and tofu, and stir well. Adjust the heat to maintain a gentle boil, and cook for 5 minutes, stirring occasionally. Have all the remaining ingredients handy, the vinegar mixture, cornstarch, and beaten eggs, so that you can add them one after the other to complete the soup.

4 cups chicken stock

¼ pound boneless pork

½ cup shredded carrots

½ cup bamboo shoots, cut into strips

½ cup firm tofu, cut into strips or ½ inch chunks (see Note)

2 eggs, beaten well

2 teaspoons Asian sesame oil

2 tablespoons thinly sliced green onion

✳ With the soup boiling gently, add the vinegar mixture and stir well. Add the cornstarch mixture and stir until the soup thickens, less than 1 minute. Stir so that the soup is whirling gently around the pan, and slowly drizzle the eggs onto the surface of the soup, so that they spread lazily out into threads.

✳ Remove from the heat, gently stir in the sesame oil and green onion, and serve hot or warm.

NOTE *If you can't find firm tofu, see page 178 for instructions on making it at home.*

chicken & eggs

Chinese cooks and diners adore chicken, and the range of dishes made with it seems endless. Many of the chicken dishes we love in Chinese restaurants can be made at home with excellent results. The four stir-fried chicken dishes with which this chapter begins are justifiably popular, and when you have your stir-fry routine in place, you will be amazed at how simple they are to cook.

My list of Chinatown restaurant favorites starts with the trio of Moo Goo Gai Pan (page 50), Almond Chicken (page 49), and Chicken with Cashews (page 55). The methods are similar, with chicken chopped or sliced, a seasoning mixture stirred up for adding near the end of the cooking time, and a session or two of chopping vegetables and herbs, like ginger, garlic, and green onions, or celery, peppers, and onions, perhaps. You can do all this in advance and refrigerate the chicken, so that when it's time to cook, you line up the ingredients at the stove and make the moves that bring together a wonderful dish.

Kung Pao Chicken (page 53) is more elaborate, though my version is streamlined enough to keep it in the quick-and-easy and delicious realm. You could substitute shrimp with great results here and amp up the chilies if you want extra heat. Lemon Chicken (page 56) is also a bit more involved, though not difficult. You'll need to slice chicken breast thinly and pan-fry it just before cooking. The sauce can be made in advance and kept warm, and the cooking is straightforward and spectacular with its sweet and tangy citrus flavors.

If you want a fix-ahead chicken dish, turn to Red-Cooked Chicken (page 60), which can be made well in advance and which only improves in flavor given time to rest before serving. Everyday Egg Foo Yong (page 62) and Taiwan-Style Omelet with Crunchy Pickled Radish (page 64) are fast and satisfying examples of the Chinese appreciation of eggs as a worthy and versatile ingredient that should never be exiled to the breakfast or brunch menu section. And for the ultimate busy-day egg dish, simply scramble three eggs, season with a bit of salt, a splash of sesame oil, and a handful of chopped fresh herbs or green onion, and cook it in a skillet as a flat omelet to enjoy with hot sauce and rice, anytime, day or night.

ALMOND CHICKEN

My father always orders this tasty Chinatown classic whenever he treats us to a family-style Chinese restaurant feast. Also known as almond *gai ding*, it's a beautiful tumble of chunky shapes. A big bowl of rice and a platter of carrot sticks and celery sticks with Sweet-and-Sour Dipping Sauce (page 172) round it out into a wonderful home-cooked meal.

12 ounces boneless, skinless chicken breast

2 tablespoons soy sauce

¼ cup chicken stock

1 tablespoon dry sherry or Shaoxing rice wine

2 teaspoons cornstarch

1 teaspoon Asian sesame oil

½ teaspoon sugar

2 tablespoons vegetable oil

2 teaspoons chopped fresh ginger

½ cup chopped onion (½-inch chunks)

½ cup chopped green bell pepper (½-inch chunks)

⅓ cup sliced bamboo shoots

¾ cup dry-roasted, salted almonds

¼ cup chopped green onion

✳ Chop the chicken breast into 1-inch chunks. Place the chicken in a medium bowl, add the soy sauce, and stir to season it evenly.

✳ In a small bowl, combine the chicken stock, sherry, cornstarch, sesame oil, and sugar, and stir well to dissolve everything into a smooth sauce.

✳ In a wok or a large, deep skillet, heat the vegetable oil over high heat. Add the ginger and toss well. Add the chicken and spread it out into a single layer. Cook undisturbed until the edges turn white, about 1 minute, and then toss well.

✳ Add the onion and green pepper. Cook, tossing now and then, until all the chicken has changed color and the onions and peppers are fragrant and beginning to wilt. Add the bamboo shoots and cook, tossing often, until the chicken is cooked through, about 1 minute more.

✳ Add the chicken stock mixture, pouring it in around the sides of the pan. Toss well to mix everything together. As soon as the sauce thickens, add the almonds and green onion and toss just until everything is evenly mixed together. Transfer to a serving plate and serve hot or warm.

SERVES 4

MOO GOO GAI PAN

I remember my first order of *moo goo gai pan* at Jung's Chinese Restaurant in Greensboro, North Carolina. It was a delectable mound of spring-green snow peas with sliced mushrooms and chicken, all glistening in a velvety sauce. I loved it then and I still do, especially since nowadays it's made with fresh mushrooms instead of canned ones.

½ pound boneless, skinless chicken breast

3 tablespoons chicken stock or water

1 tablespoon soy sauce

1 tablespoon dry sherry or Shaoxing rice wine

1 tablespoon cornstarch

1 teaspoon salt

½ teaspoon sugar

¼ teaspoon freshly ground pepper

2 tablespoons vegetable oil

1 tablespoon chopped garlic

SERVES **4**

✳ Cut the chicken breast crosswise into strips about 2 inches long. In a small bowl, combine the chicken stock, soy sauce, dry sherry, cornstarch, salt, sugar, and pepper, and stir to dissolve everything into a smooth sauce. Set out a medium bowl in which to place the chicken after its first cooking session.

✳ Heat a wok or a large, deep skillet over high heat. Add the vegetable oil and swirl to coat the pan. Add the garlic and ginger and toss well until fragrant. Scatter in the chicken, spreading it out into a single layer. Cook undisturbed until the edges turn white, about 1 minute, and then toss well. Cook until most of the pieces have changed color, and then scoop up the partially cooked chicken, leaving the liquid behind in the pan, and place into the reserved bowl.

✳ Scatter the mushrooms into the pan, spread them out, and cook for 1 minute, tossing once or twice. Return the chicken and any juices in the bowl to the pan, toss well, and cook 1 minute more.

1 tablespoon chopped fresh ginger

1 cup thinly sliced fresh mushrooms

1 cup trimmed fresh snow peas

½ cup sliced water chestnuts

2 teaspoons Asian sesame oil

✳ Add the snow peas and water chestnuts and toss well. Cook, tossing often, until the snow peas are bright green and just tender, and the chicken is cooked through.

✳ Add the chicken stock mixture, pouring it in around the sides of the pan. Cook, tossing now and then, until the sauce is bubbling, shiny, and thickened and evenly mixed with all the ingredients, about 1 minute more.

✳ Add the sesame oil, toss once more, and transfer to a serving platter. Serve hot or warm.

KUNG PAO CHICKEN

This wildly popular dish has a longer ingredients list than many of the recipes in this book, but this is mostly a matter of measuring out the two seasoning mixtures. Once that's done, there's a bit of chopping and then you're ready to cook up a speedy and spectacular dish. To prepare in advance, chop the chicken, stir up the marinade, and mix it with the meat. Cover the bowl and refrigerate it for several hours or as long as overnight. Then mix the sauce, gather the remaining ingredients, and cook. Classic recipes include Szechuan peppercorns, but if you don't have them, it's still a delicious dish.

FOR THE CHICKEN MARINADE

¾ pound boneless, skinless chicken breast

1 tablespoon soy sauce

1 tablespoon dry sherry or Shaoxing rice wine

1 tablespoon cornstarch

1 teaspoon vegetable oil

continued on next page

SERVES **4**

✳ To prepare the chicken: Chop it into bite-sized chunks, about 1 inch in diameter. In a medium bowl, combine the soy sauce, sherry, cornstarch, and vegetable oil. Stir to mix everything well, and then add the chicken, tossing to coat it evenly. Set aside for 30 minutes to 1 hour, or cover and refrigerate for up to 1 day.

✳ To make the sauce: In a small bowl, combine the soy sauce, sherry, vinegar, sugar, cornstarch, and salt. Stir to dissolve the dry ingredients, and mix everything together well.

✳ Prepare the remaining ingredients, and place everything by the stove, along with a serving platter for the finished dish.

✳ To cook the chicken, heat a wok or a large, deep skillet over medium-high heat, and then add the vegetable oil. Swirl to coat the pan, and when it is hot but not smoking, add the chiles. Toss well for about 30 seconds, and then add the Szechuan peppercorns, if using. Cook for about 1 minute, until fragrant and shiny, tossing once or twice.

FOR THE SAUCE

1 tablespoon soy sauce

1 tablespoon dry sherry or Shaoxing rice wine

1 tablespoon red wine vinegar or Chenkiang vinegar

1 tablespoon sugar

1 teaspoon cornstarch

1 teaspoon salt

FOR COOKING THE CHICKEN

2 tablespoons vegetable oil

5 to 10 small dried hot red chiles or 2 teaspoons red pepper flakes

1 teaspoon Szechuan peppercorns, toasted and crushed (optional)

1 tablespoon coarsely chopped garlic

1 tablespoon finely chopped fresh ginger

¼ cup coarsely chopped green onion

¾ cup roasted, salted peanuts

1 teaspoon Asian sesame oil

✳ Scatter in the chicken and let it cook on one side for about 1 minute. Toss well, and then add the garlic, ginger, and green onion. Cook 1 to 2 minutes, tossing now and then, until the chicken has changed color and is cooked through.

✳ Stir the sauce, and add it to the pan. Cook another minute, tossing often, and then add the peanuts and sesame oil. Toss once more, transfer to a serving platter, and serve hot or warm.

CHICKEN WITH CASHEWS

Made with chunks of chicken and celery tumbled with delectable cashews, this dish makes great party fare. It's a fine potluck contribution as well if you fill a portable serving dish with rice or pasta and scoop your Chicken with Cashews right out of the hot pan as soon as it's done. You can use chicken breast or thigh, or a combination of the two.

2 tablespoons dry sherry or Shaoxing rice wine

2 tablespoons water

1 tablespoon soy sauce

2 teaspoons cornstarch

½ teaspoon sugar

½ teaspoon salt

2 celery stalks

¾ pound boneless, skinless chicken breast or thighs, or a combination

2 tablespoons vegetable oil

2 teaspoons chopped garlic

2 teaspoons chopped fresh ginger

1 cup dry-roasted, salted cashews

3 tablespoons chopped green onion

SERVES **4**

✳ In a medium bowl, combine the sherry, water, soy sauce, cornstarch, sugar, and salt, and stir to dissolve the dry ingredients and mix everything into a smooth sauce.

✳ Trim the celery stalks, discarding tops and ends, and pull away the top layer of strings. Cut each stalk in half lengthwise, and then crosswise into ½-inch pieces; you'll need ¾ cup. Chop the chicken into big, bite-sized chunks, about 1 inch in diameter.

✳ Heat a wok or a large, deep skillet over high heat. Add the oil and swirl to coat the pan. Add the garlic and ginger and toss well until they are shiny and fragrant, about 30 seconds.

✳ Scatter in the chicken, spreading it out into a single layer. Cook undisturbed until the edges change color, about 30 seconds, and then toss well. Cook, tossing often, until most of the chicken has changed color.

✳ Add the celery, and cook, tossing often, until the celery is bright green and the chicken is cooked through, 1 to 2 minutes more. Add the sherry mixture, pouring it in around the sides of the pan, and toss well.

✳ Add the cashews and green onion. Toss to mix them in evenly and season well. Transfer to a serving plate and serve hot or warm.

LEMON CHICKEN

I love lemon chicken, but making a batter-fried restaurant-style version at home is too much mess and work. Quickly sautéed slices of chicken breast make for a delicious and doable home adaptation, with a bright-flavored sauce you can enjoy with other dishes as well. Since it takes several steps and is best served hot, this dish is one to make when you've got a little time or some helping hands, or best of all, both. Partially frozen meat is easiest to cut into thin slices, but don't worry; just do the best you can and expect delicious results.

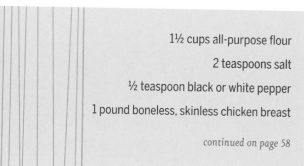

1½ cups all-purpose flour

2 teaspoons salt

½ teaspoon black or white pepper

1 pound boneless, skinless chicken breast

continued on page 58

SERVES **4**

✳ Combine the flour, salt, and pepper in a medium bowl, and stir with a fork or a whisk to mix everything well. Cut the chicken breast crosswise and on the diagonal, to make wide, thin pieces. Dip each piece of chicken into the flour to coat it well, and then gently shake off any excess. Arrange floured chicken pieces on a large plate and set by the stove.

✳ To make the lemon sauce: Combine the water and cornstarch in a small bowl and stir well. In a medium saucepan, combine the chicken stock, sugar, ginger, if using, soy sauce, and salt. Bring to a gentle boil over medium heat, and stir to dissolve the sugar and salt and mix well. Stir in the lemon juice, and as soon as the sauce is boiling gently again, add the cornstarch. Cook, stirring often, as the sauce turns cloudy, then clear, and thickens to a shiny, glossy state, about 1 minute. Remove from the heat, cover, and keep warm while you prepare the chicken.

FOR THE LEMON SAUCE

2 tablespoons water

1 tablespoon cornstarch

1 cup chicken stock

⅓ cup sugar

2 teaspoons chopped fresh ginger (optional)

1 teaspoon soy sauce

½ teaspoon salt

⅓ cup freshly squeezed lemon juice

FOR COOKING THE CHICKEN

About ⅓ cup vegetable oil

3 tablespoons thinly sliced green onion

✳ To cook the chicken, heat the oil in a large, deep skillet over medium-high heat, until a pinch of flour dropped into the oil blossoms at once. Cook in batches, placing pieces of chicken in the oil (they should sizzle immediately), and leaving a little room between so you can turn them easily and avoid crowding the pan.

✳ Cook until golden brown, 1 to 2 minutes. Turn and cook on the other side until golden and crisp, and cooked through, and then transfer the cooked chicken pieces to a serving platter as they are done. Cook the remaining chicken in the same way.

✳ Pour the hot lemon sauce over the chicken, sprinkle with the green onion, and serve hot.

FIVE-SPICE ROAST CHICKEN

The marinade for this dish imbues the chicken with an inviting brown hue and a luscious sweet-and-salty flavor. Chicken legs and thighs come out particularly well when cooked this way, but you could also do a whole chicken cut up, or two game hens instead. This dish tastes wonderful right away, and makes a perfect picnic lunch the day after.

⅓ cup soy sauce

3 tablespoons vegetable oil

2 tablespoons dry sherry or Shaoxing rice wine

1 tablespoon chopped garlic

2 teaspoons chopped fresh ginger

1 teaspoon five-spice powder (see page 14)

1 teaspoon sugar

½ teaspoon salt

3 pounds chicken legs and thighs, or one whole chicken cut up

SERVES 4 TO 6

✳ In a large bowl, combine the soy sauce, vegetable oil, sherry, garlic, ginger, five-spice powder, sugar, and salt, and stir to mix everything well and dissolve the sugar and salt.

✳ Add the chicken pieces and turn to coat them evenly. Cover and set aside for 1 hour or as long as overnight.

✳ To cook the chicken, heat the oven to 375°F. Arrange the chicken pieces on the rack of a roasting pan, or simply place them on a baking sheet with sides to catch the juices. Cook 25 minutes, and then remove from the oven to turn each piece over.

✳ Continue cooking until the chicken is wonderfully and evenly brown and cooked through, about 45 minutes total.

✳ Transfer to a serving platter and let rest for 10 minutes. Serve hot, warm, or at room temperature.

RED-COOKED CHICKEN

We adore this deeply flavored and colored braise with chicken thighs and legs, but you could use any combination of chicken pieces, bone in and skin on for maximum flavor and gorgeous hue. Probably called red-cooked because red is an auspicious color in Chinese tradition, the finished dish is in fact a handsome mahogany, in vivid contrast to the light-colored interior meat that's visible when you cut into a piece of red-cooked chicken. You need only brown the chicken pieces and assemble the braising ingredients to get this dish cooking. Once it is bubbling away on the stove, simply enjoy the aromas and cook some rice or noodles with which to enjoy the fabulous sauce.

2 tablespoons vegetable oil

5 green onions, trimmed and cut crosswise into thirds

5 slices fresh ginger

2 pounds chicken thighs or legs, or both

½ cup dark soy sauce

½ cup dry sherry or Shaoxing rice wine

⅓ cup Chinese-style rock sugar (see page 16) or brown sugar

1 teaspoon salt

1 star anise or 1 teaspoon five-spice powder (optional; see page 14)

SERVES 4

✳ Heat a large, deep skillet or a wok over medium-high heat. Add the vegetable oil and heat until a bit of green onion sizzles at once when tossed into the oil. Add the ginger slices and green onion and cook, tossing occasionally, until they release their fragrance and the green onion wilts, about 3 minutes.

✳ Scoop out and transfer the ginger and green onion to a large saucepan. Add several chicken pieces to the skillet without crowding the pan. Let them cook undisturbed until golden brown on one side, about 3 minutes. Turn to cook the other side, and then transfer to the pot, placing them on top of the green onion and ginger. Brown the remaining chicken pieces, then transfer with the cooking oil left in the skillet to the saucepan.

NOTE *You can make a tasty version with brown sugar, but rock sugar from a Chinese market is an extraordinary plus to the flavor of this dish. It keeps indefinitely, so stocking up at an Asian store or ordering a box or two via mail (see page 186) is worth a little time if you love this dish. You also need dark soy sauce, which can be bought and kept indefinitely, for color as well as flavor. If you don't have dark soy sauce, you can make a good version with ⅓ cup soy sauce and 3 tablespoons molasses in its place.*

✳ Add the dark soy sauce, sherry, rock sugar, salt, and star anise, if using, to the saucepan, and stir gently to mix them a little. Bring to a gentle, lively boil over medium-high heat, and then adjust the heat to maintain a gentle boil. The sauce should be moving visibly, but not bubbling noisily.

✳ Stir to dissolve the rock sugar and salt, and continue cooking, uncovered, stirring once or twice, for 1 hour, until the chicken is tender, cooked through, and tinged a gorgeous brown all over. Remove from the heat and set aside, so that the chicken can cool completely in the braising liquid. You can serve it after a 10-minute rest, transferring the chicken to a serving plate and providing a small bowl of the braising sauce on the side to enjoy on the chicken or over rice. Serve hot, warm, or cold, with the chicken whole or sliced.

✳ To serve later, let the chicken and sauce cool completely, and then cover and refrigerate the chicken in the braising liquid for up to 3 days. Reheat very gently in the braising liquid, heating it through without further cooking.

EVERYDAY EGG FOO YONG

Chinese restaurants in the West often feature egg *foo yong* as a plump, golden-brown pancake, studded with shrimp, barbecued pork, and bean sprouts, and served with a satiny brown sauce. This is my weeknight version, a vegetarian recipe to which you could add about ¾ cup chopped cooked shrimp, ham, crabmeat for a more substantial dish. I use smaller amounts of oil than the classic dish calls for and cook it in varying shapes. I use a wok or small skillet to cook three small omelet cakes, which I place overlapping each other on a small platter, or fold in half and fan out as three plump omelets. If I'm in a hurry, I use a large skillet to make one big flat omelet. We love this with hot sauce or salsa, but I've included a brown sauce recipe for a classic finishing touch.

3 tablespoons vegetable oil

2 teaspoons chopped garlic

¾ cup shredded carrots

¾ cup shredded napa cabbage

¼ cup chopped green onion

2 tablespoons chopped fresh cilantro

2 tablespoons soy sauce

½ teaspoon sugar

3 eggs, beaten well

1 teaspoon Asian sesame oil

1 teaspoon salt

Brown Sauce (optional; page 176)

SERVES **4**

✳ Heat a wok or a medium skillet over high heat. Add 1 tablespoon of the vegetable oil and swirl to coat the pan. Add the garlic and toss until fragrant.

✳ Add the carrots and toss until they are shiny and beginning to soften, about 15 seconds. Add the napa cabbage and green onion and toss well.

✳ Add the cilantro, soy sauce, and sugar, and cook, tossing often, until the cabbage and carrots are just tender, 1 to 2 minutes more. Transfer to a plate and spread it out into a single layer to help it cool quickly.

✳ Meanwhile, combine the eggs, sesame oil, and salt in a medium bowl. Stir with a fork to combine everything well. When the carrot mixture is no longer steaming, add it to the eggs and stir quickly to prevent the eggs from sticking and mix everything well. (If using the Brown Sauce, make it now and keep warm until serving time.)

✷ To cook the omelets, use either a wok or a small, deep skillet, so that you can make plump pancakes. (You could also cook as one big flat pancake then fold over for serving.) Heat the wok or skillet over high heat. Add about one-third of the remaining oil and swirl to coat the pan. Add about one-third of the egg-vegetable mixture and tilt the pan to spread it out a little. Fold down the edges gently as they set, and keep swiriling to encourage uncooked egg to contact the pan. Shake the pan to loosen the omelet.

✷ When the omelet is mostly set, flip it over to cook the other side. Cook until the omelet is set in the center, and then transfer to a serving plate. Repeat to make two more omelets, and serve hot or warm with Brown Sauce on the side, if using.

TAIWAN-STYLE OMELET with crunchy pickled radish

We order this simple, tasty omelet first thing whenever we can find it in Chinese restaurants. It may not be on the menu, but if someone in the kitchen hails from Taiwan and loves country cooking, you may be able to enjoy it that very night. It's easy to make, the only small challenge being to lay in a supply of *sah poh*, or pickled white radish, a sweet-and-salty preserved vegetable enjoyed throughout Asia. Serve this along with Meatball Soup with Spinach (page 37) and rice, or as a vegetarian main course with Everyday Green Beans (page 119) and rice or noodles.

½ cup finely chopped Chinese-style pickled radish (*sah poh*)

3 tablespoons vegetable oil

1 tablespoon chopped garlic

3 eggs

1 teaspoon Asian sesame oil

¼ teaspoon salt

¼ teaspoon sugar

¼ cup chopped green onion

SERVES 4 TO 6

✳ Put the chopped pickled radish in a medium bowl and add warm water to cover it. Let stand 10 minutes, and then drain well.

✳ Heat 1 tablespoon of the vegetable oil in a wok or a large, deep skillet over medium-high heat. Add the garlic and toss well until it releases its fragrance, about 15 seconds.

✳ Add the drained pickled radish, and cook, tossing often, until the radish is heated through, about 1 minute. Transfer to a plate and set aside to cool a little.

✳ In a medium bowl, combine the eggs, sesame oil, salt, and sugar. Use a fork or a whisk to mix everything together evenly and well. Stir in the green onion and the pickled radish mixture, including any liquid. Place by the stove, along with a slotted spoon or spatula for straining the egg.

✻✻✻

NOTE *This omelet is often made with lots of oil, which causes it to puff up and turn a handsome golden brown. Look for the pickled white radish, known in Taiwanese as sah poh, in cellophane packages in Asian markets or via mail order (see page 186). Transfer it to a jar to store at room temperature after opening it.*

✻✻✻

✳ Heat the remaining 2 tablespoons vegetable oil over medium-high heat. When a bit of egg blossoms at once, add about two-thirds of the egg mixture, pouring slowly and using the slotted spoon or spatula to keep most of the pickled radish mixture in the bowl while allowing egg to flow into the hot pan.

✳ Let the egg bloom and begin to cook in the hot oil. As soon as the outer edges are puffy and set, lift them up in places to allow most of the eggs to run out into contact with the hot pan. Shake the pan and lift the edges of the eggs to ensure that the omelet is browning nicely but not sticking or burning.

✳ Add the remaining egg to the pan, pouring it on top of the omelet. Carefully flip the omelet over, cooking the other side for about 1 minute more. When the second side is set and nicely browned, transfer to a serving plate and serve hot or warm.

beef

Within the Chinese culinary tradition, beef is something of a newcomer, given that the raising of cattle was traditionally limited to working animals such as oxen and water buffalo. Recipes for beef abound within the Chinese restaurant repertoire, and you will be pleased with how well you can make them at home.

My favorite cuts for stir-fry cooking include sirloin tip, tri-tip, and flank steak. You can use any tender beef cut, slicing it against the grain into thin slices about 2 inches by 1 inch. I've used less expensive cuts which are chopped into chunks for stew or kebabs, with very tasty results as well. You may see meat cut into strips for stir-fry or fajitas, and these will work, although they tend to be rather thick and might benefit from a little further slicing if you find them a bit tough.

To get thin slices at home, place the meat in the freezer for 30 minutes or so, until it is partially frozen and can be thinly sliced easily. Or defrost frozen meat, keeping track of your timing so that you get to slice it when it is about three-quarters of the way thawed, giving you the same texture which takes to slicing well.

These dishes make constant use of the seasonings and ingredients that anchor your Chinese-recipe pantry, from soy sauce and Asian sesame oil to oyster sauce, dark soy sauce, cornstarch, and sherry or Shaoxing rice wine. If you can keep these basic seasonings handy on your counter, or perhaps in a caddy you can easily set out at cooking time, you'll be ready to cook these recipes anytime.

Start with Beef in Oyster Sauce (page 81), Mongolian Beef (page 73), or Sesame Beef (page 76), none of which calls for much chopping. For a one-dish supper over rice or noodles, enjoy Beef with Broccoli (page 69) or Pepper Steak (page 70).

Orange Beef (page 74) lets you put unusual flavors on the table easily, and Spicy Beef in Lettuce Cups (page 79) help you fire up your menu in a delicious way. All are hearty and so tasty that you will want to enjoy them often.

BEEF WITH BROCCOLI

A delicious classic combination found in Chinese restaurants around the world, this dish makes a fantastic one-bowl supper over rice. With its luscious sauce, it works nicely, too, tossed with hot pasta. In Asia the green of choice would be *gai lan*, also known as Chinese broccoli, a delicious, sturdy member of the cabbage-broccoli family, in which flowers are minor and stem and leaves are the stars. To make the broccoli florets, cut the broccoli in half lengthwise unless they are very small.

¼ cup chicken stock or water

2 tablespoons oyster sauce

1 tablespoon soy sauce

½ teaspoon dark soy sauce or molasses (optional)

½ teaspoon sugar

2 tablespoons water

2 teaspoons cornstarch

2 tablespoons vegetable oil

2 teaspoons chopped garlic

2 teaspoons chopped fresh ginger

½ pound thinly sliced beef

3 cups broccoli florets

SERVES **4**

✳ In a medium bowl, combine the chicken stock, oyster sauce, soy sauce, dark soy sauce, if using, and sugar, and stir to make a smooth sauce. In a small bowl, combine the water and cornstarch.

✳ Heat a wok or a large, deep skillet over high heat. Add the oil and swirl to coat the pan. Add the garlic and ginger and toss until they release their fragrance.

✳ Add the beef, spreading it out into a single layer. Cook undisturbed until the edges change color, about 30 seconds. Toss well, and then add the broccoli florets. Cook 1 minute, tossing once, until they are shiny and bright green.

✳ Add the chicken stock mixture, pouring it in around the sides of the pan. Cook, tossing often, until the broccoli is tender and the beef is done, 2 to 3 minutes.

✳ Add the cornstarch mixture to the center of the pan. Toss to combine everything well, and as soon as the sauce thickens, transfer to a serving plate. Serve hot or warm.

PEPPER STEAK

A Chinese American restaurant standard, this combination of sweet bell peppers and tender beef is justifiably famous. Usually prepared with green bell peppers, it looks beautiful with a mix of red, yellow, orange, and green peppers and tastes great either way. I add freshly ground pepper to my basic version and toss in a teaspoon of chopped hot chile peppers, fresh or dried, if we're hungry for a little heat. You can use any tender beef sliced thinly, but I especially love rib eye or tri-tip for this dish.

1 tablespoon dry sherry or
Shaoxing rice wine

1 tablespoon water

2 teaspoons cornstarch

½ pound thinly sliced beef

2 tablespoons soy sauce

1 tablespoon chicken broth or water

1 teaspoon dark soy sauce or
molasses (optional)

1 teaspoon salt

½ teaspoon granulated sugar

½ teaspoon freshly ground pepper

continued on page 72

* Combine the sherry, water, and cornstarch in a medium bowl, and stir well to dissolve the cornstarch. Add the beef and stir to season it evenly with the sauce. Set aside for 15 minutes.

* In a small bowl, combine the soy sauce, chicken broth, dark soy sauce, if using, salt, sugar, and pepper, and stir to mix well. Place a medium bowl by the stove to hold the bell peppers after their initial cooking.

* Heat a wok or large, deep skillet over high heat. Add 1 tablespoon of the oil, and swirl to coat the pan. Add the garlic and ginger and toss well.

* Scatter in the bell peppers and toss again. Spread them out into a single layer and cook undisturbed for 15 seconds. Then, cook, tossing often, until they are shiny and just beginning to wilt, about 30 seconds more. Scoop them out into the bowl and set aside.

* Let the pan heat up again briefly, and then add the remaining 2 tablespoons oil, swirling to coat the pan again.

SERVES **4**

3 tablespoons vegetable oil

1 tablespoon chopped garlic

2 teaspoons chopped fresh ginger

2 cups thinly sliced green bell pepper strips (or red, yellow, or mixed colors)

✳ Add the beef and its marinade, spreading the beef out into a single layer. Cook undisturbed for 30 seconds, and then toss well. Cook, tossing often, until most of the meat is no longer pink, about 1 minute.

✳ Return the bell pepper and any juices in the bowl back to the pan, and toss well.

✳ Add the soy sauce mixture, pouring it in around the edges of the pan. Cook, tossing often, until the peppers are tender but not limp and the beef is cooked through, about 1 minute more. Transfer to a serving plate and serve hot or warm.

MONGOLIAN BEEF

This hearty stir-fry delivers the wintry flavors of China's northern and western provinces, where hoisin sauce, sesame oil, and other intensely flavored seasonings abound. You'll need about a cup of chopped green onions, making them more like a vegetable than an accent. This recipe works wonderfully with lamb and provides enough sauce to be tossed with pasta. For a little heat, stir in Toasted Szechuan Peppercorns (page 176) along with the green onions.

2 tablespoons soy sauce

1 teaspoon cornstarch

¾ pound thinly sliced beef

1 tablespoon hoisin sauce

1 tablespoon dry sherry or Shaoxing rice wine

½ teaspoon dark soy sauce

1 teaspoon sugar

½ teaspoon salt

10 green onions

2 tablespoons vegetable oil

1 tablespoon chopped garlic

½ teaspoon Asian sesame oil

SERVES **4**

✳ In a medium bowl, combine the soy sauce and cornstarch and stir well, until you have a smooth, caramel-brown sauce. Add the thinly sliced beef and toss to coat evenly. Set aside for 10 minutes.

✳ In a small bowl, combine the hoisin sauce, sherry, soy sauce, sugar, and salt, and stir to mix well and dissolve the sugar and salt.

✳ Trim the green onions and halve them crosswise, separating green portions from white ones. Quarter white portions lengthwise, and then chop them crosswise into 1-inch lengths. Chop the green tops crosswise into 1-inch lengths. If the green tops are thick and sturdy, halve them lengthwise before cutting them crosswise.

✳ Heat the vegetable oil in a wok or a large, deep skillet over high heat. Add the garlic and toss well. Add the beef and its marinade, spreading the beef out into a single layer and letting it cook for 30 seconds undisturbed. Toss well, and then add the green onions. Cook, tossing often, until the beef has changed color and the green onions are shiny, fragrant, and beginning to wilt.

✳ Add the hoisin sauce mixture, pouring it in around the sides of the pan. Toss well, then add the sesame oil. Toss once more and transfer to a serving platter. Serve hot or warm.

ORANGE BEEF

Traditionally made with dried strips of orange or tangerine peel that are soaked in warm water, and then cut into thin strips, Orange Beef merits lots of rice or noodles with which to enjoy its luscious sauce. Look for dried orange or tangerine peel in small cellophane packets in Asian markets and through mail-order sources (see page 182). I've made this dish with both fresh and dried peel, and both give delicious results.

¾ pound thinly sliced beef

2 tablespoons soy sauce

2 tablespoons thinly shredded fresh orange or tangerine peel, zest, or dried orange peel (see Note)

1 tablespoon chopped fresh ginger

2 teaspoons chopped garlic

1 teaspoon red pepper flakes

SERVES **4**

✳ In a small bowl, combine the beef with the soy sauce and toss to season the meat evenly. Set aside for 10 minutes. Combine the orange peel, ginger, garlic, and red pepper flakes in a small bowl, and stir to mix them together lightly.

✳ In a medium bowl, combine the sherry, orange juice, sugar, cornstarch, dark soy sauce, and salt. Stir well to dissolve the cornstarch and mix everything into a smooth sauce.

✳ Heat the vegetable oil over high heat in a wok or a large, deep skillet. Scatter in the beef and its mariande and spread the beef out into a single layer. Let it cook undisturbed for about 15 seconds, and then toss well. Add the carrots and cook, tossing now and then, until the beef is no longer pink and the carrots are beginning to wilt, about 1 minute.

2 tablespoons dry sherry or
Shaoxing rice wine

2 tablespoons orange juice

1 tablespoon sugar

2 teaspoons cornstarch

½ teaspoon dark soy sauce

1 teaspoon salt

2 tablespoons vegetable oil

½ cup shredded carrots

½ teaspoon Asian sesame oil

3 tablespoons finely chopped green onion

✱ Add the orange peel mixture and cook, tossing often, until it releases its fragrance, about 30 seconds.

✱ Add the orange juice mixture, pouring it in around the sides of the pan, and toss well. Cook, tossing now and then, until the beef is tender and evenly seasoned with the sauce. Add the sesame oil and green onion, toss well, and transfer to a serving dish. Serve hot or warm.

•••

NOTE *To use dried tangerine or orange peel, soak a small handful of pieces in warm water until they are softened and pliable, about 20 minutes. Drain well, and slice them into very thin strips. Cut strips crosswise to make very small pieces, about ½ inch by ⅛ inch.*

You can find dried orange or tangerine peel in Asian markets in small cellophane packages. You could also dry your own, removing the peel from a tangerine in a long spiral, scraping away some of the white pith, and setting it out for 3 to 5 days to dry completely at room temperature; it will still be pliable, like leather. Then store airtight, for up to 6 months.

•••

SESAME BEEF

This recipe works wonderfully as part of a party menu. There's a quantity of meat to be thinly sliced; but once it has marinated, it needs only a quick stir-fry, since the marinade includes all the seasonings. Plan ahead so that you can leave the sliced beef in the marinade for at least an hour before cooking it, or let it marinate in the refrigerator for up to 24 hours. We love it with rice, a small platter of cucumber slices and halved cherry tomatoes, and a big salad. If toasting the sesame seeds is too much, replace them with 1 tablespoon of toasted Asian sesame paste or peanut butter, stirring it into the marinade before you add the beef.

2 tablespoons white sesame seeds or
1 tablespoon peanut butter or
Asian sesame paste

¼ cup soy sauce

3 tablespoons sugar

2 tablespoons Asian sesame oil

2 tablespoons finely chopped garlic

½ teaspoon salt

¼ teaspoon freshly ground pepper

1¼ pounds beef sirloin tip,
tri-tip, or eye of round

2 tablespoons vegetable oil

¼ cup finely chopped green onion

✳ To toast the sesame seeds, heat a small, dry skillet over medium heat. Add the sesame seeds, and let them brown gently for 1 to 2 minutes, shaking the skillet and stirring them often to avoid burning. When most of the seeds are a handsome light brown and giving off a toasty aroma, scrape them out onto a small plate to cool. (If using peanut butter or Asian sesame paste, simply add it to the marinade along with the other ingredients.)

✳ In a medium bowl, combine the soy sauce, sugar, sesame oil, garlic, salt, and pepper. Stir to dissolve the sugar and mix everything together well.

✳ Grind the toasted sesame seeds in a spice grinder, or use a mortar and pestle, to make a very coarse, seedy paste. Or pile them up on a cutting board and chop them coarsely, stopping once or twice to scrape the seeds back into a mound. Scrape the toasted sesame seeds into the soy sauce marinade, and stir to mix well.

SERVES **4** TO **6**

✳ Cut the beef across the grain into very thin slices, about 2 inches long. Transfer the sliced beef to the soy sauce marinade, turning to coat evenly. Cover and refrigerate for at least 1 hour, or as long as 24 hours, turning occasionally to season all the beef evenly. (You could combine the marinade and the beef in a resealable plastic bag and then refrigerate the bag.)

✳ To cook the beef, heat the vegetable oil in a wok or a large, deep skillet over medium-high heat until very hot. Scatter in about half the beef and spread it out in one layer to cook on one side for about 1 minute. Toss well, and then turn the pieces so that the other side can cook, for up to 1 minute, until the color changes. Add half the green onion, toss well, and transfer to a serving platter. Allow the pan to heat up again, so that a bit of meat sizzles at once. Repeat with the remaining beef and its marinade and green onion. Serve hot or warm.

SPICY BEEF in lettuce cups

This Szechuan-style dish is quite delicious, quick to prepare, and fun to eat. You can use flatter lettuce leaves, such as romaine or oak leaf lettuce, and fold them into small packets for eating. Or enjoy the filling in tortillas or pita bread, along with a handful of shredded lettuce and a dollop or two of spicy salsa. We love it with rice and greens for a weeknight supper.

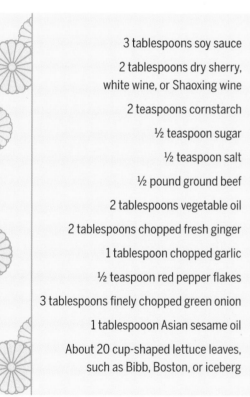

3 tablespoons soy sauce

2 tablespoons dry sherry, white wine, or Shaoxing wine

2 teaspoons cornstarch

½ teaspoon sugar

½ teaspoon salt

½ pound ground beef

2 tablespoons vegetable oil

2 tablespoons chopped fresh ginger

1 tablespoon chopped garlic

½ teaspoon red pepper flakes

3 tablespoons finely chopped green onion

1 tablespooon Asian sesame oil

About 20 cup-shaped lettuce leaves, such as Bibb, Boston, or iceberg

SERVES **4**

✳ In a small bowl, combine the soy sauce, sherry, cornstarch, sugar, and salt, and stir well to dissolve the cornstarch and combine everything into a smooth sauce.

✳ Place the ground beef in a medium bowl, and use a spoon to separate it into five or six big clumps. Add about half the soy sauce mixture, and gently mix the seasonings into the ground beef, using your hands or a large spoon. Set aside for 10 to 15 minutes.

✳ To cook, heat a wok or a large, deep skillet over medium-high heat until very hot. Add the vegetable oil; swirl to coat the pan, and then toss in the ginger and garlic. Cook for about 1 minute, tossing once, until fragrant but not browned.

✳ Crumble in the seasoned ground beef, and use your spatula or a big, slotted spoon to break it up and spread the meat out over the hot pan to help it cook evenly. Let it cook until it changes color on one side, 1 to 2 minutes.

➤ ➤ ➤

✳ Toss the meat just enough to turn the uncooked side onto the hot pan, and let it cook another minute undisturbed. Then toss well, using your spatula to break up any large chunks. When the meat is cooked, add the red pepper flakes and the green onion, and toss well. Add the sesame oil and remove from the heat, tossing once more to mix everything well.

✳ Transfer to a serving plate and serve hot, warm, or at room temperature. Arrange lettuce cups on a serving platter, and fill each one with a spoonful or two of the cooked beef. Or provide lettuce cups and the serving plate of beef and invite guests to make up lettuce packets themselves.

BEEF IN OYSTER SAUCE

Savor this hearty dish with rice and either steamed broccoli or a salad of spinach leaves or crisp romaine in a fruity vinaigrette. You could add sliced shiitakes or button mushrooms along with the carrots, or toss in a cup of tiny peas to make it a one-dish supper, serving it in bowls over rice.

2 tablespoons soy sauce

1 tablespoon dry sherry or Shaoxing rice wine

1 teaspoon cornstarch

¾ pound thinly sliced beef

2 tablespoons oyster sauce

1 tablespoon chicken stock or water

1 teaspoon sugar

½ teaspoon salt

2 tablespoons vegetable oil

2 teaspoons chopped fresh ginger

¾ cup shredded carrots

3 tablespoons thinly sliced green onion

SERVES **4**

✳ In a medium bowl, combine the soy sauce, sherry, and cornstarch, and stir to mix them well. Add the beef, toss to season it evenly, and set aside for 10 minutes. In a small bowl, combine the oyster sauce, chicken stock, sugar, and salt, and stir well.

✳ Heat the oil in a wok or a large, deep skillet. Add the ginger and toss well. Scatter in the beef and spread it out into a single layer over the surface of the pan. Let the beef cook undisturbed for 15 seconds, and then toss.

✳ Add the carrots and cook, tossing now and then, until they are shiny and softened, about 30 seconds. Add the oyster sauce mixture, pouring it in around the sides of the pan, and toss well.

✳ Cook, tossing often, until the beef is cooked and the sauce thickens and evenly coats the beef, about 1 minute more. Add the green onion and toss well. Transfer to a serving dish and serve hot or warm.

pork

Pork is the favorite meat within Chinese cooking, treasured for its richness and flavor, and the myriad ways it can be prepared. Pigs have been raised for food in China for centuries and are utilized both in home cooking and in barbecue-specialty shops, cafés, noodle shops, dim sum parlors, and banquet halls.

This chapter provides you with recipes for restaurant favorites including **Sweet-and-Sour Pork** (page 89), **Mu Shu Pork** (page 87), and **Ma Po Tofu** (page 93). My versions are streamlined to keep these classics doable in a Western home kitchen on a busy day, and I think you will find the resulting recipes to your liking.

Boneless pork tenderloin is lean and easy to use, but it can also be dry. I often buy pork shoulder, pork butt, pork chops, or country-style ribs, dividing them into half-pound portions to freeze for future use.

I hope you will also try several of the less-familiar dishes that don't show up as often outside of communities where Chinese customers know their delights. **Lion's Head Meatballs** (page 95), a simple and completely delicious casserole of gargantuan pork meatballs simmered with delectable Asian greens, is perfect with rice as the centerpiece for supper on a wintry night.

Char Shiu Pork (page 98) is a definite make-in-advance item, but once you've marinated it and roasted it in the oven, you will have a versatile and luscious ingredient on hand for noodle dishes, sandwiches, and fried rice. Of course, you can simply serve it sliced and stir-fried with a dash of sesame oil to be eaten with **Bok Choy Stir-Fried with Garlic** (page 120) and rice or noodles. Pork with *char shiu* flavors is a quick route to the sweet, salty, and rich flavors of Chinese-style barbecued pork.

Pork with Black Bean Sauce (page 92) is a rustic classic sure to become popular at your table. **Salt-and-Pepper Pork Chops, Taiwanese-Style** (page 85) are fantastic and fast, a memorable dish to share with family and friends.

SALT-AND-PEPPER PORK CHOPS, taiwanese-style

When my family arrives at the Taipei airport after our long journey from our North Carolina home, our first stop after baggage claim is the noodle shop located outside the main arrivals hall, en route to the bus ticket counters. Its menu of hearty, comforting street-food meals reminds us that the long journey was worthwhile and marks the beginning of another happy reunion with my husband's family. In the original dish, a thin-cut bone-in pork chop is served atop a bowl of soup noodles or a small mountain of rice. I like to present it on a serving of **Everyday Noodles with Sesame Oil** (page 143). Plan ahead so that these delicious Taiwanese-style pork chops have an hour or more to marinate before cooking time.

3 tablespoons soy sauce

2 tablespoons cornstarch

1 tablespoon sugar

¼ teaspoon salt

1 teaspoon freshly ground pepper

1¼ pounds boneless, thin-cut pork loin chops (see Note)

2 tablespoons vegetable oil

SERVES 4

✳ In a medium bowl, combine the soy sauce, cornstarch, sugar, salt, and pepper. Stir well to dissolve the sugar and cornstarch, and mix everything together into a smooth and flavorful marinade.

✳ Add the pork chops, turning to coat them evenly, and then cover and refrigerate for 1 hour, and up to 24 hours, turning now and then to season them well.

✳ To cook the pork chops, heat a large skillet over medium-high heat until very hot. Add the oil and swirl it to coat the pan well.

✳ Add the pork chops and their marinade in batches, cooking 1 to 2 minutes per side, until they are golden brown and cooked through. Transfer to a serving platter and serve hot or warm.

●●●

NOTE *To use bone-in thin-cut pork chops, buy about 1¾ pounds and allow a little extra cooking time.*

●●●

MU SHU PORK

I adore this northern Chinese–style dish, whether we eat it tucked into **Mandarin Pancakes** (page 179) seasoned with a little hoisin sauce or enjoy it as part of a rice-centered meal. *Mu shu* means "cassia blossom," a delicate yellow flower which is suggested by the puffy chunks of softly scrambled eggs in the dish. This is my weeknight version of the classic dish, in which I've included fresh mushrooms, shredded napa cabbage, and carrots. I've omitted the traditional dried lily buds and cloud ear mushrooms, which require soaking and trimming before cooking.

½ pound thinly sliced pork (such as pork shoulder, pork butt, or thick-cut pork chops)

2 tablespoons soy sauce

3 tablespoons chicken stock

2 tablespoons dry sherry or Shaoxing rice wine

1 teaspoon salt

½ teaspoon sugar

2 tablespoons water

2 teaspoons cornstarch

3 tablespoons vegetable oil

2 large eggs, beaten well

continued on next page

✳ Cut the pork crosswise, against the grain, into thin slices. Stack the slices and cut them lengthwise into shreds. Put the pork in a medium bowl, add the soy sauce, and toss to season it evenly. Set aside for 10 minutes.

✳ In a small bowl, combine the chicken stock, sherry, salt, and sugar, and stir to mix everything well. In another small bowl, combine the water and cornstarch and stir to mix evenly, leaving the spoon in the bowl so you can give it a final stir. Place a medium bowl by the stove to hold the eggs after they are scrambled.

✳ Heat a wok or a large, deep skillet over high heat. Add 1 tablespoon of the vegetable oil, and swirl to coat the pan.

✳ Add the eggs, and swirl to spread them out over the surface of the pan. Cook until the edges begin to set, and then gently pull them in and lift them up to expose most of the liquid to the hot pan. Toss gently, scooping and turning to let the eggs cook into soft, moist lumps. Transfer the eggs to the bowl and set aside. (Underdone is better than dry, as it will go back into the pan at the end of cooking.)

SERVES 4

1 tablespoon chopped garlic

2 teaspoons finely chopped fresh ginger

¾ cup shredded carrots

¾ cup thinly sliced fresh mushrooms

2 cups shredded napa cabbage or
3 cups baby spinach leaves

2 teaspoons Asian sesame oil

¼ cup finely chopped green onion

❀❀❀

NOTE *Though the pork for this dish is traditionally shredded into thin strips, sliced pork works fine. Instead of button mushrooms, you can use 3 ounces of fresh shiitakes. Cut away and discard the stems, and then cut their caps into thin strips, about ¼ inch wide, to make about 1 cup.*

❀❀❀

✳ Let the pan heat up again, and then add the remaining 2 tablespoons vegetable oil. Swirl to coat the pan. Add the garlic and ginger and toss well until fragrant. Add the pork and spread it out into a single layer. Cook 30 seconds undisturbed, and then toss well.

✳ Add the carrots and mushrooms and toss well. Cook, tossing often, until the pork has changed color, and the carrots and mushrooms are shiny and softening, 1 to 2 minutes. Add the napa cabbage and cook, tossing often, until it brightens in color and begins to soften, about 1 minute more.

✳ Add the chicken stock mixture and cook, tossing often, until the pork is cooked through and the vegetables are tender but not limp, 1 to 2 minutes more. Give the cornstarch mixture a good final stir, add it to the pan, and toss well just until the sauce begins to thicken.

✳ Add the sesame oil and green onion, along with the scrambled eggs, and toss gently, just to mix everything well. Transfer to a serving platter and serve hot or warm.

SWEET-AND-SOUR PORK

This recipe captures the sparkling flavors of classic sweet-and-sour dishes, without the heaviness and effort of frying battered chunks of pork. You'll want lots of rice, noodles, couscous, or grains with which to savor the sauce. You can make this with chicken, shrimp, or tofu, adjusting the cooking time according to which protein you choose. The ingredient list looks long, but once you cook the simple sweet-and-sour sauce and stir together the seasonings for the pork, you'll be just a toss or two away from an extraordinarily delicious and beautiful dish.

2 tablespoons dry sherry or
Shaoxing rice wine

1 tablespoon soy sauce

1 teaspoon salt

FOR THE SWEET-AND-SOUR SAUCE

2 tablespoons water

2 teaspoons cornstarch

¼ cup chicken stock or vegetable stock

2 tablespoons white vinegar

2 tablespoons sugar

2 tablespoons ketchup

1 tablespoon pineapple juice from canned
pineapple chunks, or orange juice

continued on next page

✻ In a small bowl, combine the sherry, soy sauce, and salt and stir well.

✻ To make the sweet and sour sauce: In a small bowl, combine the water and cornstarch, and stir to mix them well. Set aside. Combine the chicken stock, vinegar, sugar, ketchup, and pineapple juice in a small saucepan. Stir with a fork or a whisk to combine everything well. Bring to a gentle boil over medium heat and cook 1 minute. Stir in the cornstarch mixture and cook just until the sauce becomes shiny and thickened. Remove from the heat and keep warm.

✻ Set a serving platter by the stove, to hold the peppers and onions after their initial cooking, as well as the finished dish.

SERVES 4

FOR THE PORK

2 tablespoons vegetable oil

1 tablespoon chopped fresh ginger

2 teaspoons chopped garlic

¾ cup coarsely chopped
red and green bell peppers

½ cup coarsely chopped onion

½ cup canned or fresh pineapple chunks

8 ounces thinly sliced pork

3 tablespoons chopped green onion

✳ Heat a wok or a large, deep skillet over high heat. Add the oil and swirl to coat the pan. Add the ginger and garlic, toss well, and cook until fragrant, about 15 seconds. Add the bell peppers and onions and cook, tossing often, until fragrant and beginning to wilt. Add the pineapple and cook 1 minute more. Scoop the mixture onto the serving platter, leaving as much liquid behind as possible, and set aside.

✳ Let the pan heat up again, and scatter in the pork. Spread it out into a single layer, and cook undisturbed until the edges change color, about 30 seconds. Toss well and cook, tossing often, until most of the pork is no longer pink.

✳ Add the sherry–soy sauce mixture and toss well. Return the bell pepper mixture to the pan and toss to mix everything together well. Add the sweet-and-sour sauce and cook, tossing often, until all the ingredients are evenly seasoned. Add the green onion and toss again. Transfer to a serving platter and serve hot or warm.

PORK WITH BLACK BEAN SAUCE

Salty meets smooth in this classic stir-fry combination pairing the richness of pork with the salty counterpoint of fermented black beans. You'll mix three different seasonings prior to cooking this dish, but once you've done that, the dish comes together quickly. We love this with **Egg Flower Soup** (page 38) and lots of rice to capture every bit of irresistible black bean sauce.

3 tablespoons chicken stock or water

2 tablespoons dry sherry or Shaoxing rice wine

2 tablespoons water

1 tablespoon soy sauce

2 teaspoons cornstarch

1 teaspoon sugar

¾ pound thinly sliced pork

2 tablespoons coarsely chopped fermented black beans

2 tablespoons chopped fresh ginger

2 teaspoons chopped garlic

2 tablespoons vegetable oil

¾ cup 2-inch strips green bell pepper

2 tablespoons chopped green onion

2 teaspoons Asian sesame oil

SERVES 4

✱ Combine the chicken stock, sherry, and water in a small bowl, and stir well and set aside. Combine the soy sauce, cornstarch, and sugar in a medium bowl, and stir to dissolve the cornstarch and sugar. Add the pork, stir well, and set aside for 15 minutes.

✱ Combine the black beans, ginger, and garlic in another small bowl. Stir well to combine into a coarse paste.

✱ Heat a wok or a large, deep skillet over high heat. Add the vegetable oil and swirl to coat the pan. Add the pork and spread it out into a single layer. Cook undisturbed until it changes color around the edges, about 30 seconds, then toss. Continue cooking, tossing occasionally, until no longer pink, about 1 minute more.

✱ Add the bell pepper strips and cook, tossing often, until they are shiny and beginning to wilt, about 1 minute. Add the black bean mixture and toss well. Add the chicken stock mixture and cook, tossing occasionally, until the sauce comes to a gentle boil.

✱ When the pork is cooked through, the peppers are tender, and the seasonings combine into a smooth sauce, add the green onion and sesame oil, toss well, and transfer to a serving plate. Serve hot or warm.

MA PO TOFU

With its plush texture and complex flavors, this dish is a favorite with my family. I use firm tofu, but soft tofu works fine, too. It may crumble a bit, but that suits the texture of this dish. If you don't have hot bean sauce or Szechuan peppercorns, don't worry; you can still make a tasty version without them. If you can't find firm tofu, see page 178 for instructions on pressing soft tofu into firm tofu.

1 pound firm tofu

2 tablespoons hot bean sauce or
1 tablespoon hoisin and
1 tablespoon chili-garlic sauce

2 tablespoons soy sauce

½ teaspoon dark soy sauce or
molasses (optional)

1 teaspoon sugar

1 teaspoon salt

2 tablespoons water

continued next page

SERVES 4

✳ Chop the tofu into ½-inch chunks and set aside. In a small bowl, combine the hot bean sauce, soy sauce, dark soy sauce, if using, sugar, and salt. Stir well to mix them into a smooth sauce. In another small bowl, combine the water and cornstarch. Stir well to dissolve the cornstarch, leaving the spoon in the bowl for a final stir.

✳ Heat a wok or a large, deep skillet over medium-high heat, and add the vegetable oil. Swirl to coat the pan evenly. Add the garlic, ginger, and half the green onion, and toss until they release their fragrance.

✳ Add the pork, and use your spatula or a large spoon to chop and press it out into a single layer. Let it cook undisturbed until the edges change color, about 30 seconds. Toss well and cook until most of the meat has changed color, about 1 minute more.

2 teaspoons cornstarch

2 tablespoons vegetable oil

1 tablespoon chopped garlic

1 tablespoon chopped fresh ginger

¼ cup chopped green onion

½ pound ground pork

⅓ cup chicken stock

1 teaspoon Asian sesame oil

1 teaspoon **Toasted Szechuan Peppercorns** (optional; page 176)

✳ Add the hot bean sauce mixture and cook, tossing often, until the meat is evenly seasoned. Add the chicken stock and the tofu and cook, tossing gently now and then, until the pork is cooked through, 1 to 2 minutes more.

✳ Give the cornstarch mixture a final stir and add it to the pan. Toss well to mix in and let it thicken the sauce, about 15 seconds. Remove from the heat and quickly add the sesame oil, Szechuan peppercorns, if using, and remaining green onion. Toss well, transfer to a serving plate, and serve hot or warm.

◓◓◓

NOTE *Tofu is sometimes sold in 14-ounce containers, and one of those will be sufficient to make this dish. Hot bean sauce is a chile-fired version of brown bean sauce, a thick, salty seasoning made from salted, fermented soybeans. You can mix equal parts of brown bean sauce or hoisin with chile-garlic sauce for a good substitute in many recipes.*

◓◓◓

LION'S HEAD MEATBALLS

No lions here—just oversized pork meatballs (a lion's head) simmered with napa cabbage (his flowing mane) in a tasty broth. Even if you don't see the resemblance, you will love the satisfying simplicity of this dish. Cooking time is long, but once you've assembled the meatballs and put the dish on simmer, the work is done and the reward is worth the wait. You can make this in a wok, a large Dutch oven, or a Chinese-style clay pot, either on top of the stove or in the oven.

FOR THE MEATBALLS

2 tablespoons soy sauce

1 tablespoon dry sherry or
Shaoxing rice wine

1 teaspoon salt

1 beaten egg

1 pound ground pork

3 tablespoons chopped green onion

2 teaspoons finely chopped fresh ginger

continued on next page

SERVES 4

✳ To make the meatballs: In a large bowl, combine the soy sauce, sherry, salt, and egg. Stir well with a fork or a whisk to combine everything evenly. Add the ground pork, green onion, and ginger. Using your hands or a wooden spoon, mix the meat and seasonings to combine them smoothly and very well. Shape into 4 plump balls, and flatten each one slightly, like big, rounded burgers. Set aside on a plate.

✳ To make the soup: Trim the napa cabbage, discarding the outer leaves. Quarter it lengthwise, and then chop it crosswise into 2-inch lengths. Measure out 6 cups of cabbage pieces into a large bowl, reserving any remaining cabbage for another dish. In a medium bowl, combine the chicken stock, soy sauce, sugar, and salt and stir to dissolve the sugar and salt.

▶ ▶ ▶

FOR THE SOUP

1 medium head napa cabbage
(about 1 ¼ pounds) or bok choy

½ cup chicken stock

1 tablespoon soy sauce

½ teaspoon sugar

½ teaspoon salt

2 tablespoons vegetable oil

NOTE *If you want to use a casserole dish, you can brown the meatballs and cabbage in a wok or skillet and transfer them to the casserole. If it is safe for stovetop use, you could brown them in the casserole. To cook in the oven, place the assembled dish of cabbage, meatballs, and seasonings in a 300°F oven and cook for about 1 hour, until the meatballs are cooked through. Transfer to a serving bowl or serve directly from the casserole.*

✽ In a wok, heat the oil over medium-high heat until a bit of cabbage sizzles at once. Add two of the meatballs and cook on one side until nicely browned, about 2 minutes. Gently turn them over and brown the other side well. Carefully return the partly cooked meatballs to the plate, and brown the other two in the same way.

✽ Let the oil heat up again, and then add the chopped napa cabbage. Cook, tossing now and then, until the cabbage is shiny and beginning to soften, 1 to 2 minutes. Remove from the heat and return about half the cabbage to the bowl.

✽ Carefully place the four meatballs on top of the cabbage in the wok, and cover them with the remaining leaves. Add the chicken stock mixture, return the pan to the stove, and bring to a gentle boil over medium-high heat.

✽ Adjust the heat to maintain a gentle simmer, cover, and cook 30 minutes, until the meatballs are done and the cabbage is tender. Remove from the heat and transfer to a large serving bowl. Serve hot.

CHAR SHIU PORK

Bright red on the outside and lusciously salty-sweet in its flavor, Chinese-style barbecued pork is Asian fast food at its best. Home cooks, street vendors, and restaurateurs buy it by the pound from Chinese barbecue shops, which also sell roast duck, roast chicken, and roast pork, among other items. *Char shiu* pork is a versatile ingredient enhancing stir-fries, soups, and noodle dishes. Thinly sliced and tossed in a hot pan with ginger and garlic and a little oil, it makes a terrific quick meal over rice, with sliced cucumbers on the side for a cool, green crunch. My home-style version lacks the delicious charred flavor bestowed by a professional oven, as well as the red food coloring which creates its trademark color, but it makes an absolutely wonderful and useful dish.

2 tablespoons soy sauce

2 tablespoons hoisin sauce

2 tablespoons ketchup

2 tablespoons dry sherry or
Shaoxing rice wine

2 tablespoons dark brown or
light brown sugar

1 tablespoon finely minced garlic

2 teaspoons dark soy sauce or molasses

1 teaspoon paprika

MAKES ABOUT **1** POUND BARBECUED PORK

✳ In a large bowl, combine the soy sauce, hoisin sauce, ketchup, sherry, brown sugar, garlic, dark soy sauce, and paprika. Stir with a whisk or a fork to combine everything evenly and well.

✳ Cut the pork with the grain into long, plump strips, about 2 inches in diameter. (Boneless country-style ribs are just the right size already.) Immerse the pork strips in the soy sauce mixture and turn to coat them evenly. Cover and refrigerate for at least 1 hour and as long as 8 hours.

✳ To cook the pork, heat the oven to 375°F. Place an ovenproof rack on a roasting pan, and add water to a depth of ½ inch in the pan. Remove the pork from the soy sauce mixture, and place the strips on the rack over the water, several inches apart. Roast for 30 minutes.

2 pounds boneless pork, preferably
fatty pork shoulder, pork butt, or
country-style pork ribs

¼ cup honey

2 tablespoons hot water

NOTE *You can use pork tenderloin in this recipe, but the meat will be a little drier and less rich than a classic version of char shiu pork. Reduce the cooking time, as it will be done faster than fattier cuts of pork. If you like, you can reserve the marinade and baste the pork before you turn it midway through the cooking process.*

✳ Reduce the heat to 350°F, and turn the pork pieces over to cook them evenly. Cook for about 20 minutes more.

✳ While the pork is cooking, combine the honey and hot water in a large bowl, and stir to mix them well.

✳ When the pork is done, remove from the oven and dip each strip into the warm honey glaze. Set aside to cool to room temperature. To serve, slice thinly across the grain. To keep, leave the pork pieces whole, and cover and refrigerate them for up to 5 days. Or freeze them, whole and well wrapped, for up to 1 month.

fish & shellfish

You know already that fish and shellfish cook quickly, but you may not know how extraordinarily delicious they can be when prepared the Chinese way. Principle number one for Asian cooks in general is that the edible treasures harvested from rivers and oceans should be left alone as far as possible, to show off their natural flavors and textures.

This means that fish and shellfish can all be part of your busy-day menus. Start with shrimp, which make the most beautiful stir-fry of all in my opinion, and for the smallest amount of effort compared to slicing meat and stirring together complex sauces. Shrimp with Tiny Peas (page 103) is gorgeous; it's dazzling enough for a party and simple enough for supper in a bowl over rice.

Shrimp with Zucchini and Sweet Red Peppers (page 106) makes a speedy supper on a hot summer night when you don't want too much stove time before dinner. A stop at the farmers' market will give you peppers and zucchini, and ripe tomatoes and crisp cucumbers that you can slice and dress with salt and pepper to call it a meal. If you can find them at the beach or elsewhere, purchase flavorful wild-caught shrimp; buy a supply to freeze for stir-fries, or for Grilled Ginger Shrimp (page 104), in the days ahead.

Here you'll find outstanding dishes featuring fish, from Pan-Fried Snapper with Aromatic Soy Sauce (page 107) and Halibut Steamed with Fresh Ginger (page 109) to Salmon with Ginger and Onions (page 111). Clams with Black Bean Sauce (page 115) taste fabulous with the traditional accompaniment of rice, or as a pasta dish, scooped onto a plate of linguine for an Eastern spin on the Italian classic.

Shrimp Egg Foo Yong (page 112) is a traditional dish that combines shellfish with eggs. The results are delicious and will convince you that eggs shouldn't be exiled to the breakfast menu, as we tend to do in the West.

In addition to these recipes for the fish and shellfish beloved within Chinese cuisine, consider some of the sauces in the basics chapter at the end of the book as accompaniments for your standard repertoire of fish and shellfish. Next time you're grilling salmon or tuna steaks, or sautéing big, sweet scallops, or preparing freshly caught trout or bluefish, cook them simply the way you know and love, and then give them a quick-and-easy Chinese finish with a fantastic, flavorful dip or sauce.

SHRIMP with tiny peas

This dish of plump pink shrimp dotted with spring-green peas is the quintessential stir-fry: simple in concept, short on ingredients, and long on flavor. You can use regular-sized frozen peas, or edamame beans, instead of petite peas. Fresh peas work beautifully if you cook them in advance of adding them to the pan, so that they are tender when the shrimp is done.

2 tablespoons vegetable oil

1 tablespoon coarsely chopped garlic

¼ cup coarsely chopped onion

½ pound medium shrimp, peeled and deveined

2 teaspoons soy sauce

1 teaspoon sugar

1 teaspoon salt

1 cup frozen tiny peas

¼ cup chicken broth or water

2 tablespoons thinly sliced green onion

SERVES 4

✳ In a wok or a large, deep skillet, heat the oil over medium-high heat. Add the garlic and toss well. Add the onion and cook 1 minute, tossing once or twice.

✳ Scatter in the shrimp and spread them out in a single layer to cook on one side for about 1 minute more. Toss well, and then let the shrimp cook on the other side for about 30 seconds.

✳ Add the soy sauce, sugar, salt, and peas, and then toss well. Add the chicken broth and cook 1 to 2 minutes more, until the shrimp are just cooked through. Scatter in the green onion, toss once more, and transfer to a serving plate. Serve hot or warm.

GRILLED GINGER SHRIMP

A simple ginger-soy marinade seasons shrimp in less than one hour, and a brief blast of heat—whether it's a quick turn on the grill, in a grill pan, or in a hot oven—bestows fantastic flavor and color. I love these with Tangy Plum Sauce (page 174), but they're wonderful with a great salsa or a spicy-hot dipping sauce. I like to leave the tails and first joint of the shell on, while breaking off and discarding the small pointed piece attached at the base of the tail. Leaving the tail on helps you turn the shrimp with tongs while they are cooking on the grill and adds beautiful color as well. You could also thread the marinated shrimp onto bamboo skewers, about three per skewer, before or after cooking.

1 tablespoon finely chopped fresh ginger

2 teaspoons chopped garlic

1 tablespoon soy sauce

½ teaspoon Asian sesame oil

½ teaspoon sugar

½ teaspoon salt

1 pound medium shrimp, tails left on but peeled and deveined

Tangy Plum Sauce (page 174) or **Sweet-and-Sour Dipping Sauce** (page 172)

✳ In a medium bowl, combine the ginger, garlic, soy sauce, sesame oil, sugar, and salt, stirring well to dissolve the sugar and salt. Add the shrimp and turn to season them evenly with the marinade. Cover, and place in the refrigerator for 30 minutes or as long as 2 hours.

✳ To cook the shrimp, place them on skewers if using, or on the lightly oiled surface of a hot grill. Cook 2 minutes on one side, and then turn to cook the other side for 1 to 2 minutes more. Cut into a large shrimp at its plumpest part to see whether it is cooked through completely.

✳ Transfer the shrimp to a serving plate and serve hot or warm with Tangy Plum Sauce or Sweet-and-Sour Dipping Sauce.

SERVES 4 TO 6

SHRIMP with zucchini and sweet red peppers

This stir-fry tastes like summer and brings vivid color to the table even on a cool fall day. It's lovely with rice and a fruit salad, or pair it with couscous or with **Everyday Noodles with Sesame Oil** (page 143).

1 tablespoon soy sauce

2 teaspoons dry sherry or Shaoxing rice wine

½ teaspoon salt

½ teaspoon sugar

2 tablespoons vegetable oil

2 teaspoons chopped fresh ginger

2 teaspoons chopped garlic

½ cup chopped red bell pepper (½-inch chunks)

¾ pound medium shrimp, peeled and deveined

¾ cup chopped zucchini (½-inch chunks)

3 tablespoons chopped green onion

SERVES **4**

✳ In a small bowl, combine the soy sauce, sherry, salt, and sugar, stirring well to dissolve the salt and sugar.

✳ Heat a wok or a large, deep skillet over high heat. Add the oil and swirl to coat the pan. Add the ginger and garlic and toss well. Scatter in the bell peppers and toss until shiny, fragrant, and beginning to wilt.

✳ Add the shrimp and spread them out into a single layer. Cook undisturbed until the edges change color, about 30 seconds. Toss well and then add the zucchini. Cook, tossing often, until most of the shrimp are pink, about 1 minute.

✳ Add the soy sauce mixture, pouring it in around the sides of the pan. Toss well and cook until the zucchini and peppers are tender and the shrimp are cooked through, 1 to 2 minutes more. Add the green onion and toss again. Transfer to a serving plate and serve hot or warm.

PAN-FRIED SNAPPER with aromatic soy sauce

Stir a little soy sauce and sesame oil with chopped garlic, ginger, and green onion and you've created a fragrant chorus of flavors that make a fantastic seasoning for pan-fried fish. Snapper, tilapia, flounder, or catfish fillets work well here; you could also pour the sauce over baked or grilled fish with delicious results.

1 pound red snapper, tilapia, or flounder fillets

1½ cups all-purpose flour

1½ teaspoons salt

2 tablespoons soy sauce

2 tablespoons water

1½ teaspoons red wine vinegar, apple cider vinegar, or white vinegar

1 teaspoon Asian sesame oil

1 teaspoon sugar

3 tablespoons finely chopped green onion

2 tablespoons finely chopped fresh ginger

2 teaspoons chopped garlic

About ⅓ cup vegetable oil

SERVES **4**

✳ Cut the fish crosswise into 2-inch pieces and set aside on a plate. In a medium bowl, combine the flour and salt and stir with a fork or a whisk to combine them well. Set out a serving plate with a small bowl and spoon on it, in which to present the sauce.

✳ Dip the fish fillets into the seasoned flour and coat them well. Shake off any excess flour, return the fish to the plate, and place it by the stove.

✳ In a medium bowl, combine the soy sauce, water, vinegar, sesame oil, and sugar. Stir to dissolve the sugar and mix everything well. Stir in the green onion, ginger, and garlic. Transfer the sauce to the serving bowl on the serving platter and set aside.

✳ Just before serving time, cook the fish. Heat the vegetable oil in a medium skillet over medium-high heat until a pinch of flour dropped in to the oil blooms at once. Carefully add about half the fish and let it cook on one side undisturbed until golden brown, 2 to 3 minutes. Turn the fish to cook on the other side for about 2 minutes more.

✳ When the fish fillets are done, transfer them to the serving plate. Repeat with the remaining fish pieces. Spoon some sauce over each piece and serve at once.

HALIBUT STEAMED with fresh ginger

Cantonese cuisine focuses on fresh ingredients with a particular appreciation for seafood, and delicacy is a hallmark of many classic Chinese dishes. Banquets and family feasts often include a whole flounder, steamed and seasoned with fresh ginger, green onions, and an aromatic dollop of Asian sesame oil. I love this weeknight version, using halibut, snapper, cod, or any other meaty fillets. Use a standard Asian steamer if you have one, or improvise a steaming setup (see Note, page 110). My instructions here are lengthy because the process for steaming fish is unfamiliar to many cooks, but all the steps are simple and the resulting dish is delicious.

2 tablespoons soy sauce

2 tablespoons dry sherry or Shaoxing rice wine

2 teaspoons Asian sesame oil

2 tablespoons vegetable oil

¾ pound halibut fillets, or another meaty fish such as cod or snapper

½ teaspoon salt

2 tablespoons shredded fresh ginger

3 tablespoons thinly sliced green onion

SERVES 4

✳ In a small bowl, combine the soy sauce, sherry, and sesame oil, and stir well. Place it by the stove for preparing the sauce right after cooking. Put the vegetable oil in a small saucepan or small skillet and place it by the stove as well. Set a serving plate for the fish by the stove, along with a long-handled spatula or V-shaped metal tongs with which to transfer the fish from its cooking plate to its serving plate, where you will add the seasonings.

✳ To use a standard steamer, fill the base of a steamer set or a wok with about 4 inches of water. Place the steamer basket over the water. Set out a plate that will fit inside the steamer basket, on which to place the fish.

✳ Arrange the fish skin side down on the plate. (If you have more than one piece, leave a little space between them.) Sprinkle the salt lightly over the fish. Scatter the ginger over the fish. Put the plate in position inside the basket or on the rack, and bring the steaming water to a rolling boil over high heat.

➤ ➤ ➤

⁂

NOTE *Steaming is simple once you know how, but to have great results, set up your steaming equipment completely, with water and cooking plate in place, before you turn on the heat and put the fish in place for cooking. This way you won't need to experiment or make adjustments while the steam is flowing. Long, V-shaped spring-loaded metal tongs are very useful in steaming, particularly for moving fish or a plate away from the steam. Oven mitts are another way to protect your hands. If you don't have steaming equipment, you can improvise in numerous ways. Here are several ideas.*

Create a wide, thin ring by removing both lids (and contents) from a small container, for example, such as a tuna can. Place it in the bottom of a large pot, such as a Dutch oven, which is wide enough to hold a medium plate easily. Add 3 inches of water to a large pot that is wide enough to hold a medium plate, such as a Dutch oven. Place the metal ring in the center of the pan and balance the cooking plate for the fish on the ring.

To use a wok, place it on the stove and add 3 inches of water. Place 2 sturdy chopsticks in the wok at right angles, forming an X over the water. Place the cooking plate on top of the chopsticks and make sure it is firmly balanced there before adding the fish. If you don't have a lid for the wok, simply let it cook uncovered.

⁂

✳ When the steam is flowing well, adjust the heat to maintain an even steam flow, and cover the steamer basket with its lid. Cook the fish for 10 minutes, or until it is done to your liking at the thickest part of the fish. Turn off the heat and leave the fish in the steamer while you heat the oil.

✳ Place the small pan or skillet of oil over medium-high heat. Let it heat up until it is hot but not smoking, about 1 minute. Remove from the heat and keep it handy.

✳ Carefully transfer the fish to a serving plate, leaving any liquid behind. Quickly pour the soy sauce mixture over the ginger-covered fish, and scatter the green onion on top of the ginger. Slowly pour the hot oil over the top of the fish, expecting a big sizzle and gingery aroma. Serve hot.

SALMON with ginger and onions

This recipe turns a skilletful of thickly sliced onions into a steamer of sorts for salmon fillets. When the fish is done, you simply season the onions and serve them along with the ginger-infused salmon. I like it with **Asparagus with Ginger and Sesame Oil** (page 123) and warm, crusty bread.

2 tablespoons soy sauce

1 tablespoon dry sherry or Shaoxing rice wine

1 teaspoon salt

½ teaspoon sugar

1 tablespoon vegetable oil

1 tablespoon chopped fresh ginger

2 cups thickly sliced onions

¾ pound thick salmon fillets

¼ cup chopped green onion

2 tablespoons chopped fresh cilantro leaves

SERVES 4

✳ In a small bowl, combine the soy sauce, sherry, salt, and sugar, and stir well to dissolve the salt and sugar.

✳ Heat a medium skillet with a tight-fitting lid over high heat. Add the oil and swirl to coat the pan. Add the ginger and toss well. Add the onions and cook, tossing often, until they are shiny, fragrant, and beginning to wilt, about 1 minute.

✳ Lower the heat to medium, and place the salmon on top of the onions. Pour the soy sauce mixture over the salmon fillets and then cover the skillet. Cook undisturbed for about 10 minutes, until the salmon is done.

✳ Transfer the salmon fillets to a serving plate and set aside. Increase the heat to high and toss the onions well. Add the green onion, toss once, then transfer to the serving plate and arrange the salmon fillets on top of the onions. Sprinkle with the cilantro and serve hot.

SHRIMP EGG FOO YONG

This is my variation on *egg foo yong*, which is more of a scramble than a pancake-style dish. The Chinese-American restaurant version is small plump omelets cooked to a handsome, crispy brown and served with Brown Sauce (see page 176). *Foo yong* (beautiful flower) is a reference to the delicate texture and color of eggs scrambled in this way. Enjoy this with rice and other dishes, Chinese-style, or make it part of a luscious brunch or a special occasion breakfast with hash browns and toast.

4 eggs

1 teaspoon soy sauce

½ teaspoon Asian sesame oil

¼ pound shrimp, peeled and deveined

2 tablespoons vegetable oil

½ teaspoon salt

⅓ cup shredded carrots

½ cup shredded napa cabbage or bean sprouts

⅓ cup chopped green onion

SERVES **4**

✳ In a medium bowl, combine the eggs with the soy sauce and sesame oil. Stir with a fork to mix everything together well.

✳ Chop the shrimp coarsely, cutting each one into 4 to 6 pieces. (I quarter the plump top portion, and cut the tail crosswise into 2 or 3 pieces.) Set a medium bowl by the stove to hold the shrimp after they are cooked, along with a serving plate for the finished dish.

✳ Heat a wok or a large, deep skillet over high heat until hot. Add 1 tablespoon of the vegetable oil and swirl to coat the pan. Add the salt and stir to mix it into the oil.

✳ Add the carrots and toss to heat them in the oil. Let them cook for about 15 seconds, and then scatter in the shrimp. Toss well, and then cook undisturbed for 30 seconds.

✳ Toss again, and then add the shredded cabbage. Cook, tossing often, until the shrimp are pink and firm and the cabbage has softened a little and brightened in color, about 1 minute. Transfer to the bowl and set aside.

✳ Let the pan heat up again, and then add the remaining tablespoon of vegetable oil, swirling to coat the pan evenly. Add the eggs and let them cook undisturbed until they begin to set around the edges, about 15 seconds. Begin to scramble them gently, lifting up the cooked edges and pushing them in as you tilt the pan to let uncooked egg reach the hot surface.

✳ When the eggs are partially cooked, add the shrimp mixture with its juices, and begin to scoop and turn gently to combine the shrimp with the eggs and help the eggs cook evenly. Cook, scrambling gently, until the eggs are almost done but still very moist, about 30 seconds.

✳ Add the green onion, scoop and turn a few more times until the eggs are just done, and transfer to a serving plate. Serve hot or warm.

CLAMS with black bean sauce

Small, delicate clams such as the Manila variety are ideal for this dish. Rice goes wonderfully with any black bean–sauce dish, since you want to savor every bit of the sauce, but noodles would be a great pairing here as well. Plan to serve these hot as soon as they come out of the pan, and provide a bowl for the shells. Serve a bright-flavored cool accompaniment such as sliced tomatoes and cucumbers from your summer garden, or a simple green salad.

2½ pounds small clams in the shell (about 2½ dozen)

5 tablespoons water

2 tablespoons coarsely chopped fermented black beans

2 tablespoons dry sherry or Shaoxing rice wine

1 tablespoon oyster sauce

2 teaspoons soy sauce

½ teaspoon sugar

2 teaspoons cornstarch

1 teaspoon Asian sesame oil

2 tablespooons vegetable oil

1 tablespoon chopped garlic

1 tablespoon chopped fresh ginger

¼ cup chopped fresh cilantro leaves

2 tablespoons chopped green onion

✳ Using a stiff brush, scrub the clams well under running water. Discard any that stay open when tapped.

✳ In a small bowl, combine 3 tablespoons of the water with the black beans, sherry, oyster sauce, soy sauce, and sugar, and stir well. In another small bowl, combine the remaining 2 tablespoons water with the cornstarch and sesame oil, and stir to mix well.

✳ Heat a wok or a large, deep skillet over medium-high heat. Add the vegetable oil and swirl to coat the pan. Add the garlic and ginger, toss well, and cook for about 30 seconds. Add the clams and stir well.

✳ Add the black bean mixture and toss well. Raise the heat to high and cook, tossing occasionally, until most of the clams have opened, 5 to 6 minutes.

✳ Add the cornstarch mixture around the sides of the pan, and toss well. Cook, tossing occasionally, until the sauce is smooth and thickened. Toss once more and remove from the heat.

✳ Add the cilantro and green onion and toss again. Discard any unopened clams. Scrape clams and sauce onto a large serving platter and serve hot or warm, providing a bowl for the shells.

SERVES 4

vegetables & salads

Use this chapter to finally get around to eating vegetables, a lot of them, often, on an ongoing basis, just because they taste so good. Asian cooks love vegetables on their own terms, as interesting, unique, and potentially delicious ingredients worthy of a meaningful place at the table. They prepare vegetables with a minimum of fuss and effort, knowing when to act and when to leave things alone, when to combine several vegetables and when to focus on one ingredient.

Notice the dishes in this chapter, and how simple each one is. With the exception of **Corn with Tomatoes and Edamame Beans** (page 125), each is a starring role for one vegetable, and each has very few ingredients and a short cooking time.

You'll need lots of garlic, ginger, and green onions (each a little at a time, of course) and a steady supply (in small amounts) of salt and Asian sesame oil. You'll need a little time with knife and cutting board, to trim and chop most vegetables for these dishes. This chopping can be done in advance, leaving you ready to toss the ingredients together in a hot pan just before serving time.

You could also cook most of these dishes in advance, and then serve them warm or at room temperature. In fact many are even tasty cold, converting themselves into salad-type dishes for a picnic. They exist in Chinese cuisine to accompany rice, soup, and another dish or two or three depending on how many gather for a meal, as a salty, delicately crunchy, colorful, and fresh component of the menu. In addition, most of them can be tossed with hot noodles and perhaps a little olive oil, sesame oil, or butter if needed to create a flavorful noodle dish to accompany grilled fish, sautéed shrimp, a cool bowl of gazpacho, or creamy cucumber soup on a summery day.

Once you've done your knife work, you're minutes away from simple and wonderful stir-fried dishes like **Everyday Green Beans** (page 119) and **Asparagus with Ginger and Sesame Oil** (page 123). **Corn with Tomatoes and Edamame Beans** (page 125) looks and tastes wonderful, and works beautifully whether you use fresh, frozen, or canned corn. Stir together **Cool and Tangy Cucumbers** (page 126) whenever you want a fast, fresh note on your menu.

Once you know how to cook **Broccoli with Garlic and Ginger** (page 127), **Napa Cabbage Stir-Fried with Ginger and Green Onion** (page 122), or **Bok Choy Stir-Fried with Garlic** (page 120), you will be thinking about how simple and tasty it would be to apply your vegetable stir-fry skills to an abundance of other vegetables. Stroll through the farmers' market, or saunter by the salad bar, and see what comes to mind: bell peppers, watercress, spinach, broccoli rabe, fresh fava beans, sugar snap peas, savoy cabbage, or cauliflower can come out deliciously cooked in much the same way, quickly and easily.

EVERYDAY GREEN BEANS

Chinese cooks appreciate green beans for their straitlaced, sensible quality, cooking them with simplicity and speed. The result is a lovely pile of summery-green rods, firm to the bite and full of salty-sweet flavor. Make them often, and keep a batch cold in the fridge so that you can toss them into salads, fried rice, and pasta dishes right before they are done. They also make a dandy little snack and picnic component, along with tomato sandwiches (white bread, mayo, tomatoes, salt and pepper) and deviled eggs. On busy days, look for trimmed green beans in the produce section, bagged and ready to go.

1 pound fresh green beans

2 tablespoons vegetable oil

1 tablespoon chopped garlic

½ teaspoon salt

⅓ cup water or chicken stock

SERVES 4

☻☻☻

NOTE *If you have a lid that fits on your skillet or down inside your wok but still above the beans, put it on after adding the water to boost the heat. Check often: you may need to add a little more water if they aren't done on this schedule, and keep tossing till they are ready. Or turn them out, sauce and all, if they are done earlier. For tiny French-style haricots verts, shorten the cooking time.*

☻☻☻

✳ To prepare the green beans, trim away the ends and pull off any strings. Chop the beans crosswise into 3-inch lengths.

✳ Heat a wok or a large, deep skillet over high heat. Add the oil and swirl to coat the pan. Add the garlic and salt and toss until fragrant, about 15 seconds.

✳ Scatter in the green beans and toss well until they are shiny and starting to brighten to a vivid green. Add the water, pouring it in around the sides of the pan, and toss well. Cook, tossing now and then, until the green beans are tender but still firm and the pan is almost dry.

✳ Transfer to a serving plate and serve hot, warm, or at room temperature.

BOK CHOY STIR-FRIED with garlic

This simple home-style stir-fry has put bok choy on my weekly grocery list. Its bright white stalks and lush green leaves cook up into a remarkably delicious, pleasantly textured dish that tastes great with rice or noodles. Think of it as a delicious vegetable dish, a worthy companion to steak and baked potato, grilled salmon, or pasta tossed either with pesto, or with garlic and oil.

1¼ pounds bok choy

2 tablespoons vegetable oil

3 slices fresh ginger

2 teaspoons chopped garlic

1 teaspoon salt

¼ teaspoon sugar

2 tablespoons water

SERVES 4

✳ Trim away and discard the bottom inch or so at the base of the bok choy, along with any tired outer leaves and stalks. Quarter the bok choy lengthwise, and then line up the spears. Cut crosswise into 2-inch lengths, and transfer the pieces to a large bowl. Tumble to loosen up all the leaves and pieces; you should have around 6 cups.

✳ Heat a wok or a large, deep skillet over high heat. Add the oil and swirl to coat the pan.

✳ Add the ginger, garlic, and salt and toss well. Scatter in the bok choy and toss well, until it is shiny and beginning to wilt, less than 1 minute.

✳ Add the sugar and water and continue cooking, tossing now and then, until the leaves are vivid green and the stalks are tender but not limp, 1 to 2 minutes. Add a little more water if needed to prevent burning while cooking.

✳ Transfer to a serving plate and serve hot or warm.

NAPA CABBAGE STIR-FRIED with ginger and green onion

Also known as Chinese cabbage or celery cabbage, this long, plump member of the cabbage family cooks to a pleasing sweetness. Beloved in soups and braised dishes, it makes a delicious, quick stir-fry to accompany a rice-centered meal. If you like dried shrimp, soak a handful in warm water, chop them coarsely, and toss them in with the ginger for a salty accent to this quickly prepared vegetable dish.

1¼ pounds napa cabbage

2 tablespoons vegetable oil

3 slices fresh ginger

1 teaspoon chopped garlic

½ teaspoon salt

½ teaspoon sugar

1 tablespoon water

2 tablespoons chopped green onion

1 teaspoon Asian sesame oil

SERVES 4

✳ If you have a small head of napa cabbage, trim away 2 inches from the base and any tired outer leaves. Halve it lengthwise and then cut crosswise into 2-inch lengths. Measure about 6 cups. (If you have a large, plump head, halve it lengthwise, and then trim away the base and outer leaves from one half only, reserving the rest for another use. Halve the trimmed half lengthwise, and then cut crosswise into 2-inch lengths to get 6 cups.)

✳ Heat a wok or a large, deep skillet over high heat. Add the vegetable oil and swirl to coat the pan.

✳ Add the ginger, garlic, and salt and toss well. Scatter in the napa cabbage and toss well, until it is shiny and beginning to wilt, less than 1 minute.

✳ Add the sugar and water and continue cooking, tossing now and then, until the leaves have brightened in color and are tender but not limp, 1 to 2 minutes. Add a little more water if needed to prevent burning while cooking.

✳ Add the green onion and sesame oil and toss well. Transfer to a serving plate and serve hot or warm.

ASPARAGUS with ginger and sesame oil

Though I never heard of asparagus until I was fully grown and far from my North Carolina home, I adored it at once. Prep is as simple as snapping off the woody base of each stalk, and cooking time is short. Simply delicious hot from the pan or grill, it is also wonderful cold or at room temperature for quick suppers or a picnic lunch. Adjust cooking time to the size you find, remembering that slender stalks will cook more quickly than thick, sturdy ones will.

1 pound asparagus
(about 1 standard bunch)

2 tablespoons vegetable oil

5 thin, quarter-sized slices fresh ginger

½ teaspoon salt

¼ cup water

1 teaspoon Asian sesame oil

SERVES 4

✳ To prepare the asparagus, break off and discard the woody, pale-colored base of each stalk, about 2 inches. (Hold base in one hand and bend the stalk hard; the stalk will snap apart at the natural breaking point.)

✳ Cut the usable part of the stalks on the diagonal into 2-inch sections, setting the tips aside in a small pile and the rest in a large pile.

✳ Heat a large, deep skillet over medium-high heat for about 30 seconds. Add the vegetable oil and turn the pan to coat it evenly. Add the ginger and salt and cook, scooping and pressing the ginger and mixing the oil and salt, until the ginger is fragrant, about 15 seconds.

✳ Reserving the tips, scatter in the asparagus and toss well. Cook, tossing now and then, until shiny and bright green, about 30 seconds. Add the tips and toss to mix everything well.

✳ Add the water to the pan, pouring it in around the sides, and toss to mix well. Cook, scooping and turning now and then, until the asparagus is tender but still firm, and most of the water has cooked away, about 3 minutes. (Check by piercing with a fork to see if they are tender enough.)

✳ Add the sesame oil and then toss to season well. Turn out onto a serving plate. Serve hot or warm.

CORN with tomatoes and edamame beans

This beautiful tumble of vegetables lights up a rice-centered meal, especially if it accompanies a pink pile of **Grilled Ginger Shrimp** (page 104), or boiled shrimp with cocktail sauce. In summertime we star it in a vegetable-centric supper, with slices of sweet, ripe tomatoes and cucumbers from the garden or farmers' market, a cool green salad, and jalapeño cornbread on the side. You could use fresh corn cut right off the cob, or frozen or canned corn with delicious results.

2 tablespoons vegetable oil

2 teaspoons chopped garlic

2 slices fresh ginger

1 teaspoon salt

3 cups fresh, frozen, or canned corn kernels

1 cup frozen shelled edamame beans, baby lima beans, or tiny peas

3 tablespoons water

½ cup halved cherry tomatoes (see Note)

½ teaspoon sugar

1 teaspoon Asian sesame oil

2 tablespoons chopped fresh cilantro

✳ Heat a wok or a large, deep skillet over high heat. Add the vegetable oil and swirl to coat the pan.

✳ Add the garlic, ginger, and salt, and toss well. Add the corn and toss to mix it with the oil. Add the edamame beans and toss to mix everything together well.

✳ Add the water and cook, tossing often, until the corn and edamame beans are hot and tender. (If using fresh corn, add a little extra water and time here until it is cooked.)

✳ Add the cherry tomatoes and sugar, and toss gently to mix them in evenly and heat them just a little. Add the sesame oil and cilantro, toss well, and transfer to a serving plate. Serve hot or warm.

SERVES 4

❧❧❧

NOTE *Substitue chopped Roma tomatoes, chopping two of them coarsely and leaving behind most of their juice and seeds on your cutting board.*

❧❧❧

COOL AND TANGY CUCUMBERS

These simple pickles can be prepared in advance or assembled an hour or two before you want to enjoy them. Small rods of cucumber marinated in a tangy sesame dressing work nicely as a relish with stir-fries, fried rice, or **Pot Sticker Dumplings** (page 23). This small batch can be doubled or tripled if you're preparing for a picnic or want to keep a supply on hand.

1 pound cucumbers, preferably English (hothouse) or Kirby pickling varieties

¾ teaspoon salt, divided

1 tablespoon red wine vinegar, apple cider vinegar, or white vinegar

1 tablespoon Asian sesame oil

2 teaspoons sugar

½ teaspoon finely chopped garlic

MAKES ABOUT 2 CUPS

❦❦❦

NOTE *If you love tangy flavors, make the dressing with Chinese vinegar, either dark Chenkiang vinegar or red vinegar, both of which are made from rice. You could also use balsamic vinegar, which has a deep richness along the lines of Chenkiang. Add a little* **Hot Chili Oil** *(page 175) or chili-garlic sauce if you want a little heat in the mix*

❦❦❦

✳ Peel the cucumbers, leaving a little green on and peeling only the thinnest outer skin away if you have beautiful, fresh thin-skinned cucumbers. Trim away the ends and halve the cucumbers lengthwise. Using a spoon, scoop out and discard the seeds in the center of each cucumber half, hollowing each half out into little boats.

✳ Cut each cucumber half crosswise into 2-inch lengths, and then cut each section lengthwise into sturdy little rods, about ¼ inch wide. Place them in a medium bowl and sprinkle with ½ teaspoon of the salt. Tumble them together to distribute the salt, and set them aside for 30 minutes to 1 hour.

✳ Meanwhile, combine the remaining ¼ teaspoon salt in a medium bowl with the vinegar, sesame oil, sugar, and garlic. Stir to dissolve the sugar and salt and mix everything together well.

✳ When the cucumbers are ready, rinse them well, and then pat them dry with kitchen towels or paper towels. Add them to the bowl of vinegar-sesame dressing and stir to season them evenly. Let stand 30 minutes and serve at room temperature. Cover and refrigerate, dressing and all, for up to 3 days.

BROCCOLI with garlic and ginger

Expect two requests: a copy of the recipe and a promise to bring it to the next gathering as well. It seems much too tasty to be so incredibly simple to cook, but it is just that. Once you've got the recipe in your hands and head (and that won't take long, since it's easy and you'll want to make it again), you can put this on the table to round out any Asian-style rice-centered meal. I serve it with grilled salmon, meatloaf, and pasta carbonara, since it's as easy to put together as a simple salad and it complements almost any main course.

2 tablespoons vegetable oil

1 tablespoon chopped fresh ginger

1 teaspoon chopped garlic

1 teaspoon salt

12 ounces broccoli florets

3 tablespoons water or chicken stock

1 teaspoon Asian sesame oil

SERVES 4

✳ Heat a work or a large, deep skillet over high heat. Add the vegetable oil and swirl to coat the pan.

✳ Add the ginger, garlic, and salt, and toss well. Add the broccoli and toss until combined. Cook, tossing often, until the broccoli florets are vivid green and just starting to wilt, about 1 minute.

✳ Add the water, pouring it in around the sides of the pan. Cook 2 to 3 minutes more, tossing now and then, until the broccoli is brilliant green and tender but still pleasingly crisp.

✳ Add the sesame oil, toss well, and then transfer to a serving plate. Serve hot or warm.

rice

Rice is sustenance in China, as it is in much of Asia, and every detail of traditional Chinese cuisine reflects this essential truth. Hallmarks of Chinese cooking include the intensity of seasonings, deep appreciation of variety in textures, shapes, and colors, the importance of including soup and a wide array of dishes plain and complex in one meal, and the positioning of meat more as a seasoning or accent rather than in the starring role. All these principles presume that people will be eating bowls and bowls and bowls of plain, unseasoned rice and that lots of bites from a variety of communal dishes will make for a nourishing, pleasurable, and satisfying meal.

We love rice in that plain, simple, cooked-in-water state, and we eat rice cooked in the rice cooker several nights a week. You may do the same, or you may love rice cooked with butter and salt, or a little olive oil. You may prefer brown rice or basmati rice, or rice pilaf with chicken stock, herbs, and spices. Rice in whatever form suits you will go wonderfully with the rice-centered dishes in this book. You can also substitute bread, couscous, barley, quinoa, pasta, noodles, or potatoes, as long as you include something of substance as a companion in terms of rounding out a meal and providing a platform of sorts for the stir-fries, soups, and stews included here.

This is a chapter of rice dishes, including a basic rice recipe, which is a formula for turning raw, dry grains of rice into soft, wonderful bites of cooked rice. Cooking rice is simple, but it's also confounding and can cause frustration in wonderful cooks who can't figure out why two simple things, rice and water, can't turn into a third thing, good cooked rice, every single time.

If rice success eludes you, a rice cooker can bridge the gap, as can a coach, someone who knows how and will let you watch and will watch you over time, until you get the hang of it. You can also buy cooked plain rice from many Chinese restaurants for the asking, in quantity, and at a great price. Cooked rice keeps well and reheats beautifully in a microwave or steamer, so consider buying a supply to take home the next time you eat out. Then package it up for future rice meals if that helps you keep rice handy.

The remaining dishes include four versions of fried rice, which in Asia would always be a main course or one-dish meal, rather than an alternative to steamed rice as it is offered here. You can make fried rice as a take-along dish for potlucks and use it as a centerpiece dish for a gathering, with an array of dishes to accompany it, perhaps from the grill or from guests who bring something to share.

Rice porridge, also known as *jook*, congee, or *moi*, is beloved as a breakfast as well as a late-night pleasure throughout Asia. It is simple to make, and can serve as the main rice for any meal, as it often does in Taiwanese homes. Plan to serve it with salty tidbits such as ham, pickles, omelet strips, or roast chicken.

RICE PORRIDGE

Known as *jook* in Cantonese, *shee fahn* in Mandarin, and as congee in many English-language descriptions, this simple porridge is a mainstay of the Chinese table. *Jook* is beloved as a nourishing, easily prepared meal, ideal for small children, elderly people, and anyone who is ill. But don't wait till you're convalescing—Chinese people enjoy it as a simple breakfast, a late-night snack, and a substantial anchor to a dim sum feast. This basic version requires only a little rice and a lot of water, simmered together until the rice dissolves into a luscious soup. *Jook* comes with a selection of salty, hearty, or pungent accompaniments such as roast chicken, grilled seafood, smoked fish, salty egg or omelet strips, peanuts, chopped fresh ginger, and thinly sliced green onion. You can also serve it in place of rice or noodles to anchor an Asian-style meal.

½ cup long-grain or medium-grain rice

4½ cups water

SERVES **4** TO **6**

ä ä ä

NOTE *Medium-grain or short-grain rice is ideal for making rice porridge, but long-grain rice works nicely, and since that is our house rice, that's what I use in most cases. Some traditional versions call for less rice, more water, and a longer, slower cooking time. My version makes a thick, substantial soup, which you can thin to your liking by adding hot water gradually, just before serving time.*

ä ä ä

✳ Rinse the rice in cool water and drain well. Add the 4½ cups of water and bring to a rolling boil. Stir well and then cook at a gentle but lively boil for 10 minutes, stirring often.

✳ Adjust the heat to maintain a lively, active simmer, and cook, stirring now and then, until the rice has cooked down into a soft, thick porridge, about 45 minutes.

✳ Serve hot or warm, in small bowls with soup spoons (Chinese-style porcelain soup spoons are ideal). Or set aside to cool and refrigerate, covered, for up to 1 day. To reheat, add about 1 cup water (it will have thickened a lot) and warm very gently over medium heat, stirring often, until steaming hot.

EVERYDAY RICE

This recipe makes a pot of plain, unseasoned rice, the perfect centerpiece to a meal of Chinese dishes. You may have a rice cooker, as I do, and enjoy the ease it provides on busy days. But I suggest you learn to cook rice, so that you will be ready to do so when you find yourself wanting to cook a Chinese meal in a friend's kitchen, or on a camping trip.

1½ cups long-grain rice

2 cups water

SERVES 4

✳ In a medium saucepan, rinse the rice in several changes of cool water, then drain it well.

✳ Add the 2 cups of water to the pan and place it on the stove over medium heat. Let the rice come to a gentle boil and continue cooking until the rice begins to look dry, about 5 minutes.

✳ Stir well and then cover the pan with a tight-fitting lid. Reduce the heat to low and cook 15 minutes more. Remove the covered pan from the stove and let it stand for 10 minutes undisturbed. Uncover and stir gently to fluff up the rice. Serve hot or warm.

HAM-AND-EGG FRIED RICE

My husband, Will, makes ham-and-egg fried rice better than anybody I know. He doesn't measure or write things as he cooks, so this took a little detective work, but I finally got it down to share with you. Egg fried rice is a traditional Chinese dish, and the addition of ham is a hearty and pretty touch. This makes one fine supper on a busy Sunday evening.

4 cups cooked rice, cold or
at room temperature

2 tablespoons vegetable oil

¼ cup chopped onion

4 ounces ham, chopped (about 1 cup)

1 teaspoon salt

½ teaspoon sugar

3 well-beaten eggs

3 tablespoons chopped green onion

SERVES 4

✳ Crumble the rice so that it breaks up into individual grains for easy stir-frying.

✳ Heat a wok or a large, deep skillet over medium-high heat. Add the oil and swirl to coat the pan. Add the onion and cook, tossing often, for 15 seconds. Add the ham, salt, and sugar, and toss well.

✳ Add the eggs and then tilt the pan to help them cook. Lift the edges and turn the pan, to expose as much egg as possible to the hot pan. When the edges have set, scramble them into soft lumps.

✳ Quickly add the rice and toss to mix it with the ham and eggs evenly and well. Cook, tossing often, until the rice is hot and tender, 2 to 3 minutes more. Add the green onion and toss well. Transfer to a serving plate. Serve hot or warm.

FRIED RICE with shrimp and peas

Shrimp and peas give gorgeous color to this tasty version of fried rice. Take it to a potluck, or enjoy it as a one-dish supper. If you have leftover cooked shrimp, give them a quick toss in the hot pan before adding the rice, instead of allowing time for the shrimp to cook.

4 cups cooked long-grain rice, preferably chilled

2 tablespoons vegetable oil

¼ cup chopped onion

1 tablespoon chopped garlic

1 teaspoon salt

8 ounces medium shrimp, peeled and deveined

¾ cup frozen tiny peas

2 tablespoons finely chopped green onion

3 tablespoons chopped fresh cilantro

SERVES 4 TO 6

✳ Crumble up the rice so that it breaks up into individual grains for easy stir-frying.

✳ Heat a wok or a large, deep skillet over high heat until very hot. Add the oil and swirl to coat the pan. Add the onion, garlic, and salt, and toss until shiny and fragrant.

✳ Scatter in the shrimp, spreading them out into a single layer. Cook, undisturbed, until most of the shrimp have turned pink around the edges, about 1 minute. Add the peas and toss well.

✳ Add the rice and toss well. Cook, tossing often, until the shrimp are cooked through and the rice is hot and tender, 1 to 2 minutes more.

✳ Add the green onion and cilantro and toss to mix them in. Transfer to a serving plate, and serve hot or warm.

YANGCHOW FRIED RICE

This hearty version of fried rice is popular throughout China. Because it uses cooked meats, including shrimp, ham, and chicken, it comes together quickly and makes an appealing centerpiece dish. Bean sprouts are traditional, but if you can't find crisp ones, you can substitute shredded carrots from the produce section, or napa cabbage or iceberg lettuce cut into long, thin strips.

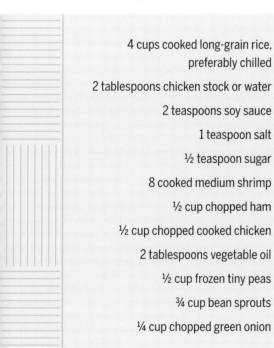

4 cups cooked long-grain rice, preferably chilled

2 tablespoons chicken stock or water

2 teaspoons soy sauce

1 teaspoon salt

½ teaspoon sugar

8 cooked medium shrimp

½ cup chopped ham

½ cup chopped cooked chicken

2 tablespoons vegetable oil

½ cup frozen tiny peas

¾ cup bean sprouts

¼ cup chopped green onion

SERVES 4 TO 6

✳ Crumble the rice, so that it breaks up into individual grains for easy stir-frying. In a small bowl, combine the chicken stock, soy sauce, salt, and sugar, and stir to dissolve the salt and sugar.

✳ Chop the cooked shrimp into small chunks, cutting each one crosswise into 4 pieces. Set aside with the ham and chicken.

✳ Heat a wok or a large, deep skillet over high heat. Add the oil and swirl to coat the pan.

✳ Add the ham and chicken and toss well. Add the chopped shrimp and cook, tossing often, to heat everything through, about 1 minute.

✳ Add the rice and toss well. Cook, tossing often, to heat and season the rice, about 1 minute. Add the chicken stock mixture, pouring it in around the sides of the pan, and toss to mix it into the rice. Add the peas and toss well.

✳ Cook, tossing often, until the rice is hot and tender and evenly seasoned, about 1 minute more. Add the bean sprouts and the green onion and toss well. Transfer to a serving platter, and serve hot or warm.

EIGHT-TREASURE FRIED RICE

In Chinese tradition, eight is a lucky number, and the "treasures" are the delicious ingredients enhancing this handsome and satisfying main-course dish. Cooking and chilling the rice a day in advance means you can easily crumble it into separate grains, the key to fluffy and flavorful fried rice. Doing your prep work (chopping ham, draining pineapple, making egg ribbons, etc.) in advance streamlines the cooking. Once the components are ready, all you need to do is toss the dish together shortly before serving time.

2 tablespoons dry sherry or
Shaoxing rice wine

1 tablespoon soy sauce

1 teaspoon salt

½ teaspoon sugar

3½ ounces fresh shiitake mushrooms or
small button mushrooms

4 cups cooked long-grain rice, chilled

3 tablespoons vegetable oil

2 eggs, beaten well

SERVES 4 TO 6

✳ In a small bowl, combine the sherry, soy sauce, salt, and sugar, and stir well to dissolve the salt and sugar. Remove and discard the stems from the shiitake mushrooms and slice the caps into slender strips. (Slice whole button mushrooms thinly lengthwise.) Using your hands, gently crumble the rice into individual grains.

✳ Heat a wok or a large, deep skillet over high heat. Add 1 tablespoon of the vegetable oil and swirl to coat the pan. Add the eggs and tilt the pan so that they spread out into a thin pancake, lifting the edges to spread it out. When set, turn and cook the other side briefly. Turn out onto a cutting board, roll into a cylinder, and slice it crosswise to make thin ribbons. Fluff and set aside.

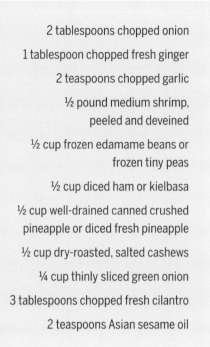

2 tablespoons chopped onion

1 tablespoon chopped fresh ginger

2 teaspoons chopped garlic

½ pound medium shrimp,
peeled and deveined

½ cup frozen edamame beans or
frozen tiny peas

½ cup diced ham or kielbasa

½ cup well-drained canned crushed
pineapple or diced fresh pineapple

½ cup dry-roasted, salted cashews

¼ cup thinly sliced green onion

3 tablespoons chopped fresh cilantro

2 teaspoons Asian sesame oil

✳ Heat the pan again over high heat. Add the remaining 2 tablespoons vegetable oil. Add the onion, ginger, and garlic and toss well. Add the shrimp and cook, tossing often, until they are firm, pink, and cooked though, 1 to 2 minutes. Add the mushrooms and edamame beans and toss until the mushrooms are shiny and softened, about 1 minute more.

✳ Add the rice and toss to mix everything well. Add the sherry seasoning mixture, pouring it in around the edge of the pan. Then add the ham, pineapple, cashews, egg ribbons, and green onion. Cook, tossing often, until the rice is hot and tender and the shrimp are cooked through, about 2 minutes more.

✳ Add the cilantro and sesame oil and toss well. Transfer to a serving platter and serve hot or warm.

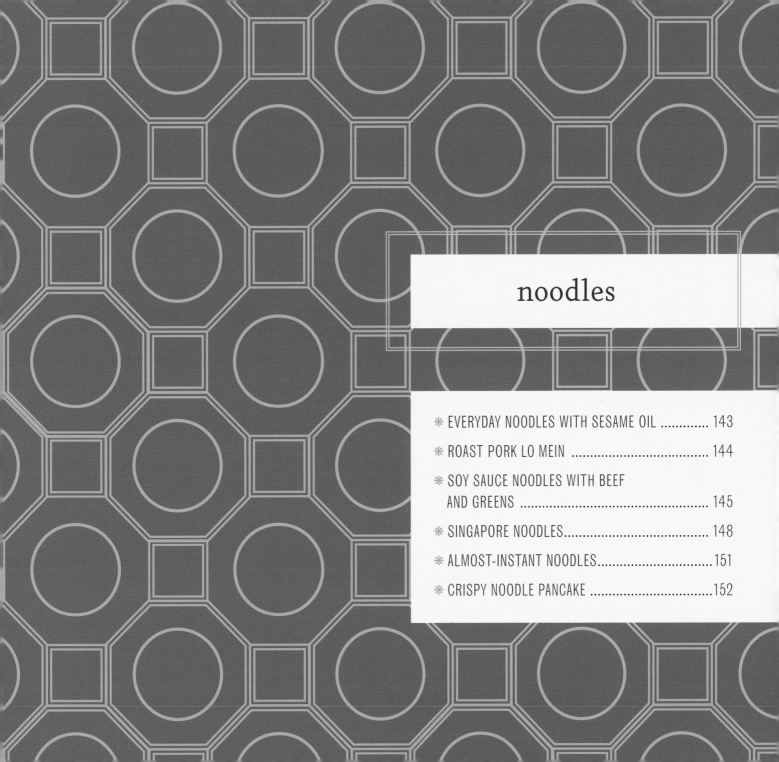

noodles

Though noodles are a mainstay of Chinese cuisine, they play a minor role in Chinese restaurants in the West. Noodle cafés abound throughout Asia, as do cooks preparing noodles in market stalls or in small boats. With a small charcoal stove and a rickety table or two, a good noodle cook can build a strong business on a corner across from the train station. Chinese noodle dishes tend to be simple and hearty, quickly made and quickly consumed, and a favorite option when dining alone.

You can make many Chinese noodle dishes at home with excellent results, and the many kinds of noodles now available in the West are a bonus to home cooks. Even supermarkets often carry dried rice noodles and bean thread noodles, as well as egg noodles and wheat noodles galore. Fresh noodles can be found in Asian markets, and all the dishes in this chapter can be made using pasta, from spaghetti and angel hair to linguine and fettucine, depending on the particular dish you want to make.

For anytime noodles to enjoy with your meal instead of rice, make **Everyday Noodles with Sesame Oil** (page 143) part of your repertoire. Lo Mein fans can get handy with **Roast Pork Lo Mein** (page 144), using it as a template for lo mein dishes, and tossing in cooked chicken, shrimp, or sausage, depending on what you like as well as what you have handy.

Soy Sauce Noodles with Beef and Greens (page 145) and **Singapore Noodles** (page 148) are two classic noodle stir-fries that you will find at many Chinese restaurants in the West. Both are standard in dim sum parlors, where people often order a platter of noodles to fill out a meal of tidbits and dumplings offered on carts. Both are delicious and doable, at their best if you prepare your ingredients ahead of time and cook them just before serving. (Though I have taken Singapore Noodles to potluck parties with excellent results.)

Completing this chapter are **Almost-Instant Noodles** (page 151), an extremely quick and simple stirred-up sauce for just-cooked noodles that can be a quick lunch, or the foundation for a toss up of cooked peas and ham. Last comes **Crispy Noodle Pancake** (page 152), a companion dish to any saucy stir-fried dish when you want a presentation piece. Try it with **Moo Goo Gai Pan** (page 50) or **Mongolian Beef** (page 73), and use a big spoon to cut chunks of noodles apart from the pancake as you serve yourself a portion.

The simplest Asian noodle dish of all is soup noodles, and for that you need no recipe. Ideally, get a big bowl (bigger than cereal size, smaller than serving size, and available in Asian markets), and put into it a good-sized clump of just-cooked pasta, such as egg noodles from an Asian market, or fresh linguine. Pour on a cup or so of wonderful chicken stock, homemade or canned but simmered with some ginger, garlic, and onion and seasoned with a dollop of sesame oil. Finish with a handful of baby spinach leaves or watercress, a sprinkling of green onion and cilantro, and a few pieces of roast chicken, ham, or cooked shrimp. You can vary the noodles, the meat, the broth; in fact, everything is mix and match, and the resulting equation is almost always one-bowl, short-notice, praiseworthy comfort food.

EVERYDAY NOODLES with sesame oil

You can serve these noodles instead of rice with any stir-fried dish. They provide a whisper of toasted sesame flavor and can be made ahead of time and served at room temperature along with grilled salmon, shrimp, kebabs, or vegetables. For a heartier noodle dish, add thin strips of ham, shreds of roast chicken, or a bowlful of cooked shrimp and toss to mix them in well. If you need to keep it for more than an hour before serving, cover and refrigerate. Then allow the noodles to return to room temperature before serving, or warm them gently in the microwave or the oven.

8 ounces thin spaghetti, angel hair pasta, or Chinese-style egg noodles

½ cup thinly sliced green onion

2 tablespoons Asian sesame oil

½ teaspoon salt

SERVES 4

✳ Bring a large pot of water to a rolling boil over high heat and add a generous pinch of salt. Add the noodles and stir to separate them as they begin to soften. Cook the noodles until just tender but still firm, 6 to 8 minutes, stirring now and then. Quickly drain, rinse with cool water, and then drain again, shaking off excess water.

✳ Transfer to a medium bowl and add the green onion, sesame oil, and salt. Toss to mix everything evenly and well. Serve warm or at room temperature.

ROAST PORK LO MEIN

Lo mein dishes are simple stir-fried concoctions of soft egg noodles, salty flavors, and tidbits of cooked meat such as Chinese-style roast pork or **Char Shiu Pork** (page 98). Use this as your basic lo mein guideline, adjusting it to your liking. You could use any kind of cooked meat or seafood, such as cooked shrimp, diced ham, or shreds of roast chicken. I love it with **Cool and Tangy Cucumber** (page 126) for a cool contrast to the luscious and hearty noodle dish.

9 ounces Chinese-style fresh egg noodles, linguine, or fettucine

1 tablespoon soy sauce

1 tablespoon oyster sauce

1 tablespoon dry sherry or Shaoxing rice wine

½ teaspoon sugar

½ teaspoon salt

2 tablespoons vegetable oil

2 teaspoons chopped garlic

2 teaspoons chopped fresh ginger

½ cup shredded carrots

1¼ cups diced **Char Shiu Pork** (page 98, or purchased), roast pork, or ham

2 cups bean sprouts or shredded napa cabbage

3 tablespoons chopped green onion

✳ Bring a large pot of water to a rolling boil over high heat and add a generous pinch of salt. Add the noodles and stir to separate them.

✳ Cook the noodles until just tender but still firm, 2 to 4 minutes, stirring now and then. (If you are using fresh pasta, cook until tender but still firm.) Quickly drain, rinse with cool water, and then drain again. You should have about 3¼ cups cooked noodles.

✳ In a small bowl, combine the soy sauce, oyster sauce, sherry, sugar, and salt, and stir well to dissolve the sugar and salt. Set aside.

✳ Heat a wok or a large, deep skillet over medium-high heat. Add the oil and swirl to coat the pan. Add the garlic, ginger, and carrot, and toss well. Add the pork and cook, tossing often, until the carrots have wilted and the pork is heated through, about 1 minute.

✳ Add the bean sprouts and the noodles and toss well to mix all the ingredients together.

✳ Add the soy sauce mixture, pouring it in around the sides of the pan. Cook, tossing often, 1 to 2 minutes. Add the green onion and toss well. Transfer to a serving plate and serve hot or warm.

SERVES 2 TO 4

SOY SAUCE NOODLES with beef and greens

Traditionally made with fresh, soft rice noodles, this dish provides a feast for your eyes with its rich, deep brown color accented by splashes of shiny and tender greens. Its natural sweetness calls for a contrasting note, so it's often served with a simple chili-vinegar sauce in noodle shops throughout Asia.

½ pound wide dried rice noodles, preferably the width of fettucine or linguine

2 tablespoons soy sauce

1 tablespoon dark soy sauce or molasses

1 teaspoon salt

3 tablespoons vegetable oil

1 tablespoon coarsely chopped garlic

½ pound thinly sliced beef

5 cups loosely packed fresh spinach leaves, or 3 cups broccoli florets

¼ to ½ cup chicken stock or water

2 eggs, lightly beaten

Chili-Vinegar Sauce (optional; page 171)

SERVES 2 TO 4

✳ Soften the dried rice noodles by dropping them into a large saucepan of boiling water. Remove from the heat at once and let stand 5 minutes, until softened and flexible but not yet tender enough to eat. Stir occasionally to separate the noodles. Drain, rinse, and drain again. Transfer to a medium bowl and place by the stove.

✳ In a small bowl, stir together the soy sauce, dark soy sauce, and salt, mixing well to dissolve the salt. Place it by the stove, spoon and all, along with a serving platter, a pair of long-handled tongs or a spatula, and a slotted spoon for tossing the noodles. Have all the remaining ingredients ready and handy.

✳ Heat a wok or a large, deep skillet over medium-high heat and add 2 tablespoons of the oil. Swirl to coat the surface, add the garlic, and toss for 30 seconds. Scatter in the beef and toss well as it begins to change color.

✳ Add the spinach and cook, tossing often, until it is shiny, bright green, and tender and the beef is cooked, 1 to 2 minutes. Transfer the beef and spinach to the serving platter.

✳ Reduce the heat to medium, scatter in the noodles, and toss well. Cook 2 minutes or so, tossing and pulling the noodles apart so that they cook evenly, and adding splashes of chicken stock as needed to keep them moist and prevent sticking. When the noodles have softened, curled up, and turned white, push them to the side of the pan.

✳ Add the remaining tablespoon of oil to the center of the pan. Pour in the eggs and swirl to spread them out into a thin sheet. When they are almost set, begin to scramble them, and then scoop and turn the noodles to mix them in.

✳ Return the beef and spinach to the pan. Add the soy sauce mixture, pouring it in around the sides of the pan, and using the spoon to get every sticky drop. Toss everything well for about 1 minute more, until the noodles are a handsome brown. Transfer to the serving platter and serve hot or warm, with Chili-Vinegar Sauce on the side, if desired.

SINGAPORE NOODLES

Singapore noodles provide an intermezzo to the tiny dumplings and tasty buns offered from carts in dim sum restaurants and are often available at other Chinese restaurants for the asking, even if they're not listed on the menu. This recipe makes a beautiful pile of tasty noodles, curry-golden and boasting plump pink shrimp and svelte green pepper strips to complete the colorful picture. You need only a few ingredients and a quick turn in a hot pan to cook it. If you like spicy heat, use a hot curry powder. You could also add a spoonful of chili-garlic sauce to the chicken-broth mixture, or provide hot sauce at the table when you serve the noodles.

One 6-ounce package dried thin rice noodles (see Note, page 150)

⅔ cup chicken stock or water

2 tablespoons curry powder

1 tablespoon soy sauce

1 teaspoon salt

4 ounces fresh shiitake or small button mushrooms

3 tablespoons vegetable oil

1 tablespoon chopped garlic

½ pound medium shrimp, peeled and deveined

1 cup chopped onion

1¼ cups thinly sliced green bell pepper

✳ Soften the dried rice noodles by dropping them into a large saucepan of boiling water. Remove from the heat at once and let stand 5 minutes, until softened and flexible but not yet tender enough to eat. Stir occasionally to separate the noodles. Drain, rinse, and drain again. Transfer to a medium bowl and place by the stove.

✳ In a small bowl, combine the chicken stock, curry powder, soy sauce, and salt, and stir well to dissolve the curry powder and salt.

✳ For shiitake mushrooms, trim away and discard their stems, and slice the caps into slender strips. (If using button mushrooms, slice them thinly lengthwise.) Set a medium bowl by the stove to hold the shrimp and vegetables during the cooking.

SERVES 2 TO 4

❁❁❁

NOTE *You may find the 6-ounce packages of dried rice noodles in the Asian section of your supermarket, as I do, along with bean thread noodles and other Asian noodle varieties. Alternatively, check Asian markets or mail-order sources (see page 182) and stock up, since these keep for a long time, just like spaghetti on your pantry shelf.*

❁❁❁

✳ Heat a wok or a large, deep skillet over high heat. Add 2 tablespoons of the oil and swirl to coat the pan.

✳ Add the garlic and toss until fragrant, about 15 seconds. Add the shrimp and spread them out into a single layer. Let them cook briefly, then toss well. Cook, tossing often, until the shrimp are firm, pink all over, and cooked through, 1 to 2 minutes. Transfer to the reserved bowl and set aside.

✳ Add the onion, green peppers, and mushrooms and toss well. Cook, tossing often, until everything is shiny, tender, and fragrant, about 1 minute more. Scoop the vegetables out of the pan and into the bowl with the shrimp.

✳ Add the remaining tablespoon of oil to the pan and swirl to coat it well. Add the noodles and toss well until they just begin to soften, about 1 minute. Add the chicken stock mixture, pouring it in around the sides of the pan, and then toss well.

✳ Return the shrimp and vegetables to the noodles in the pan and cook, tossing often, until the noodles are golden, tender, and evenly seasoned. Transfer to a serving platter, arranging a few shrimp, green peppers, and shiitake mushrooms on top of the noodles. Serve hot or warm.

ALMOST-INSTANT NOODLES

This little noodle dish makes a great lunch or snack, using the seasonings and condiments you have on hand for everyday Chinese cooking. Many supermarkets carry squarish dried wheat noodles that are curly and golden, often labeled *chukka soba* and made in Japan. You could use any cooked pasta here; the sauce will be enough for 8 to 10 ounces dried noodles, or 3 cups cooked. Add a dollop of chili-garlic sauce or hot pepper sauce if you want a little spicy kick.

2 tablespoons Asian sesame oil

2 tablespoons oyster sauce

1 tablespoon soy sauce

½ teaspoon sugar

8 ounces dried curly Asian-style noodles such as *chuka soba*, or angel hair pasta

½ cup chopped ham, roast chicken, or cooked shrimp (optional)

2 tablespoons finely chopped green onion

1 tablespoon chopped fresh cilantro

SERVES 2 TO 4

✳ In a medium bowl, combine the sesame oil, oyster sauce, soy sauce, and sugar. Stir to mix everything well and dissolve the sugar.

✳ Cook the noodles in a medium saucepan of wildly boiling water until they are just tender, 3 to 5 minutes. Drain well and transfer to the bowl of sauce.

✳ Place the ham on top, if using, along with the green onion. Toss quickly to mix and season the noodles evenly, using tongs, chopsticks, or a fork and spoon. Sprinkle with the cilantro and serve hot or warm.

CRISPY NOODLE PANCAKE

Known as "two-sides brown" in Cantonese, and as "noodle pillows" by the brilliant author and teacher Barbara Tropp, this fried noodle cake provides texture and color as the base for a saucy stir-fried dish. A favorite in dim sum parlors, the pancake calls for an abundance of oil to help it color and crisp up. In this recipe, I use a moderate amount of oil for a pleasing version that comes out as a flat pancake in a skillet and a plumper pillow in a wok. Ideally, the insides stay soft while the outer surfaces provide a crusty contrast in texture and hue. Plan ahead so that your cooked egg noodles have an hour or more to cool and dry out after you boil them and before you fry them into a crispy pancake.

8 ounces thin Chinese-style fresh egg noodles or very thin fresh pasta

5 tablespoons vegetable oil

SERVES 4

✱ Bring a large pot of water to a rolling boil over high heat and add a generous pinch of salt. Add the noodles and stir to separate them.

✱ Cook the noodles until just tender but still firm, 2 to 4 minutes, stirring now and then. Quickly drain, rinse with cool water, and then drain well. You will have about 3 cups cooked noodles.

✱ Spread the noodles out in a thin layer on a baking sheet or a tray. Let them dry out for at least one hour.

✱ When you are ready to fry the noodles, place a large skillet over medium-high heat. When it is hot, add 3 tablespoons of the oil and swirl to coat the pan evenly and well, sides as well as bottom.

NOTE *If you're making this as the foundation for a stir-fried dish, set out everything you will need for both dishes near the stove before you begin to cook. Then prepare the noodle pancake first and make the stir-fry right after that, so that you can turn the stir-fry dish out onto the noodles and serve at once. You could make the noodle pancake, set it on a heatproof serving plate, and place it in a 250°F oven for up to half an hour before you plan to serve it. If you want individual noodle cakes, you could make them quickly in a small hot skillet, shaping and cooking each one and then transferring them to a serving plate in a 250°F oven to keep warm. For more golden brown color, crispness, and firm shape, add more oil to the pan.*

✳ When a bit of noodle sizzles at once, arrange the noodles in the hot pan, spreading them out into an even layer. Cook for 6 to 8 minutes, pressing down with a spatula to form a flat, even pancake. When it is golden brown and crisp on the bottom, carefully turn it over to expose the other side to the hot pan.

✳ Add another 2 tablespoons oil, pouring it in around the edges of the pan, and let the pancake cook for 4 to 6 minutes more. When the second side is a crispy golden brown, carefully transfer the pancake to a serving plate and serve hot or warm. (Sliding it carefully onto the serving plate works well.)

sweets

Chinese cuisine holds sweetness in high esteem but, unlike most Western traditions, often joins sweet and savory rather than relegating each to its own separate domain. Sweet flavors show up alongside savory ones, throughout the meal and in street-food snacks as well as banquets and in homestyle cooking. Pork in particular is cooked with rock sugar, honey, and spices such as cinnamon, star anise, and cloves, which belong on a sweet side within Western cuisines. Additionally, sugar is often added to seasoning mixtures as a component of the flavor pattern.

Dessert as a special and anticipated course enjoyed after a festive meal is not a Chinese concept. Fresh fruit or a comforting sweet, thick soup involving small red beans, sesame seeds, poppy seeds, and rice dumplings are what you might be served on such a grand occasion. Sweet treats abound in Chinese cuisine, but most often as a snack picked up in the marketplace and brought to the teachers' lounge, bus station, or study hall, there to be nibbled with friends amid conversation.

Today, you'll find fabulous Chinese bakeries with shelves lined with gloriously decorated cakes, glistening pastries, and fruit tarts piled high with perfectly positioned berries and slices of kiwi fruit. These testify to the delight and enthusiasm with which Chinese people have embraced Western desserts and sweets, but they remain a store-bought or restaurant treat. Home ovens are rare, and the Western ingredients, techniques, and equipment used in baking present a challenge for most home cooks. Many traditional Chinese sweets are purchased from vendors to this day.

This chapter provides you with a small collection of Chinese sweets that have made themselves at home within the cuisine and can be made at home with wonderful and delicious results. Three are standards that began in the West and demonstrate a sweet and savvy harmonizing between the traditions.

Almond Cookies (facing page) and Fortune Cookies (page 160) both originate in Western lands where ovens have been standard home and restaurant equipment for generations. Almond Cookies are extremely easy to make and fortune cookies repay you well in the pleasure they provide. Egg Custard Tartlets (page 162) go back farther, to contact between China and Portugal in earliest trading days many centuries back. The Portuguese protectorate of Macau established a presence in the vicinity of Hong Kong long ago, and the traditional custard tarts of Portugal called for making a sugar syrup to be mixed with eggs and milk to make the custard. This unique method is used to this day in commercial *danh tot*, as they are called in Cantonese, and it yields extraordinarily smooth and shiny custard. You'll find them in old-style Chinese coffee shops in Chinatowns, as well as in dim sum parlors and in bakeries.

Rounding out the chapter is a Chinese-inspired dessert, elegant Five-Spice Poached Pears (page 165), which are made in advance and offer a lovely denouement to any meal.

The Chinese original of the group here is Candied Walnuts (page 166). They make a wonderful gift for your host or for friends at holidays and can be served as an after-dinner nibble or even stir-fried with shrimp or chicken, in traditional Chinese fashion, where sweet and savory dance together in delicious harmony, anytime and anyplace.

ALMOND COOKIES

This is my version of a recipe by my friend Jean Yueh, renowned cooking teacher and author of *The Great Tastes of Chinese Cooking* (see page 182). These little cookies are easy to make and eating them is a delight. Jean uses a pastry brush to glaze each cookie with a little well-beaten egg just before baking, to give them a golden sheen. You could use all butter or margarine in this recipe, if you prefer. I often make a double batch, so that I can keep a roll of almond cookie dough in the refrigerator or freezer, tightly wrapped in waxed paper or foil. That way, we can bake a batch of warm cookies anytime we want a speedy little treat.

1½ cups all-purpose flour

1 teaspoon baking powder

½ teaspoon baking soda

¼ teaspoon salt

6 tablespoons butter at room temperature, shortening, or margarine

6 tablespoons shortening or margarine

1 egg

¾ cup sugar

2 teaspoons almond extract

16 to 32 whole almonds, skinless or skin on (see Note)

MAKES **16** LARGE OR **32** SMALL COOKIES

✳ Combine the flour, baking powder, baking soda, and salt in a medium bowl and stir with a fork to mix them well.

✳ In a large mixing bowl, combine the butter, shortening, egg, sugar, and almond extract. Using an electric mixer, beat at medium speed until all the ingredients are evenly combined, 1 to 2 minutes; or use a wooden spoon to mix well.

✳ Add the flour mixture to the butter mixture and stir with a wooden spoon just enough to bring everything together into a smooth dough. Stop as soon as all the flour disappears. (If you won't be baking the cookies now, cover or wrap dough well and refrigerate it for up to 1 week, or freeze it for up to 1 month.)

➤ ➤ ➤

❀❀❀

NOTE *For larger cookies, shape each half of the dough into a cylinder about 2 inches in diameter, and cut them into a total of 16 pieces. For smaller cookies, shape each half into a cylinder about 1¼ inches in diameter, and cut them into a total of 32 pieces.*

❀❀❀

✴ Heat the oven to 400°F. Divide the dough in half and shape each half into a cylinder. (See Note about size and number of cookies.) Cut each cylinder evenly into rounds, placing each round on an ungreased cookie sheet, about 2 inches apart. Press an almond firmly into the center of each cookie, flat side up.

✴ Bake at 400°F for 10 to 12 minutes, until the cookies are firm and lightly browned. Cool on the cookie sheets, and then transfer to a serving plate, or to a cookie tin or another airtight container.

FORTUNE COOKIES

An inspiration from Chinese American restaurant traditions in the West, fortune cookies are factory made, treasured for their message, shape, and crunch rather than for flavor or ancient Chinese roots. Fellow cookbook author Sara Perry created an orange-flavored version for her wonderful book *Holiday Baking* (see page 182), and it is my good fortune that she kindly shared it with me. This is my version of her recipe. As for the fortunes, think short and sweet, and begin by writing them on slips of paper, using edible ink. For best results, Sara suggests you line your baking sheet with a reusable nonstick baking sheet liner, such as a Silpat, since it completely prevents these particularly delicate cookies from sticking to the pan.

½ cup all-purpose flour

1 tablespoon cornstarch

¼ cup sugar

⅛ teaspoon salt

¼ cup vegetable oil

2 egg whites at room temperature

1 tablespoon orange juice

1 teaspoon pure vanilla extract

1 teaspoon grated orange zest

MAKES **12** TO **16** COOKIES

✳ Heat the oven to 325°F. Line a baking sheet with a reusable nonstick sheet liner or parchment paper, and set aside. Place the fortunes, a big measuring cup, a bowl of ice water, and a 12-cup muffin tin next to the stove so that you can use them in shaping the cookies while they are hot from the oven.

✳ In a medium bowl, use a whisk or a fork to stir together the flour, corn-starch, sugar, and salt, until well and evenly blended together.

✳ Add the oil, egg whites, orange juice, vanilla, and orange zest. Using an electic mixer, beat at high speed until smooth.

❖❖❖

NOTE *Sara Perry makes these into small, elegant cylinders, rolling them up as they come off the pan. If you do it this way, you can wait and tuck a fortune into the hollow center of each cookie later, even right before serving time.*

❖❖❖

✳ Start with just 2 cookies at a time, dropping the batter by level tablespoonfuls about 3 inches apart on the baking sheet. Using the back of a spoon, spread each portion into a 4-inch diameter cookie. Bake until the edges start to brown, 8 to 10 minutes.

✳ Using a wide thin flexible spatula, lift each cookie off the baking sheet. (If it begins to tear or bunch up, let it cool for another 15 to 20 seconds. If it cools too much on the pan and won't come off, return it to the oven to resoften for about 1 minute more.)

✳ Place a fortune in the center of each cookie and quickly fold in half. Pick up one of the cookies by the rounded top, and place the folded side on the edge of the measuring cup. Press down gently to bend the folded corners down into the standard fortune cookie shape. Repeat with the other cookie, and place the shaped cookies gently in empty cups in the muffin tin to cool. (Dip your fingers into the ice water and dry them to keep them cool as you work.)

✳ Continue baking and shaping the remaining cookies. Store in an airtight container, and enjoy within 2 days.

EGG CUSTARD TARTLETS

Visit a dim sum parlor at lunchtime and you'll probably find these sunny yellow tartlets among the few sweet items offered from carts wheeled around the large, lively room. Flaky pastry cradles a silken custard in this classic Hong Kong–style dim sum item. Traditionally made with a multilayered lard pastry, these tarts can be made in a streamlined version using prepared puff pastry or pie crust. The crucial steps of making a simple syrup for the custard and baking the tartlets slowly at a low heat are easy to accomplish, so the results are simple and superb.

1 package frozen puff pastry or
1 package refrigerated pie crust
(2 crusts)

¾ cup sugar

½ cup water

4 eggs

½ cup milk

MAKES **12** TARTLETS

✳ To prepare the tartlet shells, set the frozen puff pastry dough out on the countertop and allow it to thaw until soft enough to unfold the dough. Generously grease the muffin cups in a 12-cup muffin pan. Open one of the two pieces of dough into a single layer, and cut the rectangle into 9 equal pieces, each one about 3 inches square. Open the second piece of dough and make 3 more 3-inch squares in the same way. Fold the remaining dough and freeze for another use.

✳ Using a rolling pin, roll each piece to about 4 inches square, and then place it loosely in a muffin cup. Press and shape to line the bottom and sides completely and well, letting the four points extend out above the rim. When you have lined 10 to 12 of the cups with puff pastry, set the pan in the freezer for at least 2 hours or as long as overnight. (To use prepared pie crust, cut 4-inch squares and fit them into the generously greased muffin cups, piecing and pressing them together. You will need about 1½ crusts for this dish.)

➤ ➤ ➤

✳ To make the custard filling, combine the sugar and water in a small saucepan and bring to a lively boil over medium heat. Stir well just until the sugar dissolves into a clear syrup. Remove from the heat and set aside to cool. Heat the oven to 300°F.

✳ In a medium bowl, beat the eggs very well until smooth. Add the cooled syrup and the milk and beat until everything is completely mixed together smoothly and well.

✳ When the oven is hot, remove the pastry shells from the freezer and add about 2 tablespoons of filling to each one. Bake at 300°F for 50 to 60 minutes, until the crust is golden brown and flaky and the custard is shiny and smooth and puffed up.

✳ Remove from the oven and cool in the pan to room temperature. To remove cooled pastries from the muffin pan, work each one loose from its spot in the muffin tin, using a dull table knife to break it away from the tin.

✳ Serve at room temperature, or warm.

FIVE-SPICE POACHED PEARS

Pears poached in this spiced syrup make a lovely, easy dessert. They can be made ahead of time and chilled for up to two days before serving. Make sure to choose pears that are barely ripe, firm, and unblemished. If too ripe, the pears will be mushy when poached. The poaching liquid is reduced to make a golden-spiced sauce to serve with the pears. Allow 15 minutes to reduce the sauce.

1½ cups sugar

3 cups water

1 (3-inch) piece of fresh ginger, peeled and cut into ½-inch slices

4 or 5 cloves

5 black peppercorns

1 cinnamon stick

2 or 3 star anise or ½ teaspoon five-spice powder (see page 14)

2-inch strip fresh lemon zest

½ cup dry sherry (optional)

4 firm, barely ripe pears

Caramel Ginger Sauce (optional; page 177)

SERVES **4**

✳ Combine the sugar and water in a deep saucepan large enough to hold the pear halves in a single layer, and bring to a boil over high heat to completely dissolve the sugar. Add the ginger slices, cloves, peppercorns, cinnamon stick, star anise, and lemon zest. Reduce the heat to a simmer and cook for 10 minutes.

✳ While the poaching liquid is simmering, peel the pears, leaving the stems intact. Halve lengthwise and use a teaspoon or a melon baller to scoop out the central core and interior stem.

✳ Add the sherry and the pear halves to the poaching liquid and simmer until tender but not mushy when pierced with a sharp knife, 20 to 25 minutes (the length of poaching time depends on the ripeness of the fruit).

✳ Remove from the heat and allow the pears to cool to room temperature in the liquid. Cover and refrigerate for up to 2 days.

✳ To serve, drain the pears and place on dessert plates. Strain the poaching syrup into a large saucepan and bring to a boil over high heat. Cook until the poaching liquid is reduced by half and thickens to the consistency of maple syrup, about 10 minutes. Serve the pears drizzled with the spiced syrup, or with Caramel Ginger Sauce, if using.

CANDIED WALNUTS

This simple recipe transforms tasty walnuts into crispy, sweet-tinged treats that work wonderfully as snacks or as celestial additions to stir-fried dishes. Make a lot so that you have some for nibbling, some for cooking, and some for sharing. Because you will need to move quickly with boiling water and hot sugar as you make this dish, I've given detailed directions for setting out necessary equipment before you begin cooking.

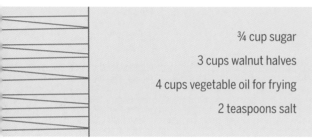

¾ cup sugar

3 cups walnut halves

4 cups vegetable oil for frying

2 teaspoons salt

MAKES ABOUT **3** CUPS

✳ In a medium saucepan over high heat, bring 6 cups of water to a rolling boil. Meanwhile, place a colander or a large strainer in the sink for draining the walnuts. Pour the sugar into a large mixing bowl and set out a large wooden spoon or a rubber spatula with which to stir the nuts. Set out a large baking sheet, for spreading out the nuts before and after frying.

✳ When the water comes to a rolling boil, add the walnuts and stir well. When they return to a boil, let them cook for 1 minute, and then drain them into the colander in the sink.

✳ Quickly transfer the walnuts to the mixing bowl, and toss and stir quickly in order to coat them evenly with the sugar. Keep stirring until they have cooled off somewhat and ceased to absorb any more sugar. Turn the sugared walnuts out onto the baking sheet, and scatter them into a single layer of nuts.

✳ To fry the sugared nuts, heat the oil in a wok or large, deep skillet over medium heat until hot, about 350°F. Have a slotted spoon or a large spoon and a strainer handy, so that you can scoop out the nuts when they are nearly done.

NOTE *Remove the walnuts from the hot oil before they are exactly the color you want because they continue cooking for a short time once they are out of the oil. Keep a few raw walnuts handy on a small plate, to help you judge how much they have colored. Things happen fast here: better to take them out early than to let them burn; they will still be delicious.*

✳ When a small piece of walnut sizzles at once, add half the sugared walnuts to the oil. Stir gently to separate them as the oil bubbles up and they begin to brown. Watch carefully, and scoop them out as soon as their color approaches a handsome golden brown.

✳ Transfer the walnuts carefully to the baking sheet and quickly spread them out in a single layer to cool completely. Repeat with the remaining sugared walnuts. When all the walnuts are cooked and cooled, sprinkle them with the salt and toss well.

✳ Transfer to an airtight container, and store at room temperature for up to 1 week.

sauces & other basic recipes

Here, you will find a repertoire of finishing touches, a line-up of delectable, intriguing sauces with which to accent recipes in this book. You'll also find instructions for preparing **Firm Tofu** (page 178), an excellent addition to stir-fried dishes and soups whether you use it as an addition to meat or in creating vegetarian dishes with Chinese flavors. It's used as an ingredient in such dishes as **Hot and Sour Soup** (page 44) and can be made easily at home for those who can't readily buy it, or who enjoy the appealing texture that the homemade version provides.

Mandarin Pancakes (page 179) are simple flatbreads, served with **Mu Shu Pork** (page 87) and Peking duck in Chinese restaurants in the West. I love their chewy texture and enjoy them with any stir-fry which isn't accompanied by lots of sauce. Try them as a small wrap for slices of **Char Shiu Pork** (page 98) or **Sesame Beef** (page 76), along with shredded lettuce and chopped tomatoes. Make them two or three times and you'll be able to do it with pleasure and ease.

The assortment of dipping sauces and seasonings are all quickly made: **Ginger-Soy Dipping Sauce** (page 171), **Chili-Vinegar Sauce** (page 171), are merely stirred together. Try the Ginger-Soy Dipping Sauce with boiled shrimp, crisp fried tofu, or grilled salmon when you want great Chinese flavor fast. **Caramel Ginger Sauce** (page 177) provides a luxurious finish to **Five-Spice Poached Pears** (page 165) and makes ice cream a dazzling treat, should you wish to enhance it with dollops of the luscious sauce.

Sweet-and-Sour Dipping Sauce (page 172), **Tangy Plum Sauce** (page 174), and **Hot Chili Oil** (page 175) each take a few minutes on the stove, but none is elaborate and each will keep for a day or two after it's made. These sauces and seasonings are all the inspiration you need to bring quick and easy Chinese flavors into your kitchen, even on busy days.

GINGER-SOY DIPPING SAUCE

This sauce is a standard accompaniment for potstickers. Vinegar and ginger provide a vibrant counterpoint to the richness of the dumplings.

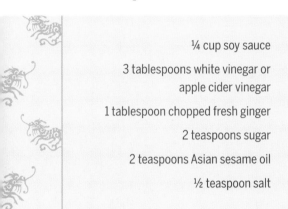

¼ cup soy sauce

3 tablespoons white vinegar or apple cider vinegar

1 tablespoon chopped fresh ginger

2 teaspoons sugar

2 teaspoons Asian sesame oil

½ teaspoon salt

✳ Combine the soy sauce, vinegar, ginger, sugar, sesame oil, and salt in a medium bowl. Whisk or stir well to dissolve the sugar and salt, and mix everything together into a thin, smooth sauce.

MAKES ABOUT ½ CUP

CHILI-VINEGAR SAUCE

This simple condiment provides a satisfyingly sharp contrast to the rich, dark flavors of **Soy Sauce Noodles with Beef and Greens** (page 145) and other dishes. The hot chiles can be serranos, jalapeños, or even tiny Thai chiles if you love hot and spicy flavors.

½ cup white vinegar

½ teaspoon soy sauce

2 tablespoons chopped or thinly sliced fresh hot green chiles

✳ Combine the vinegar, soy sauce, and chiles in a small bowl, and stir well. Cover and refrigerate for up to 1 week.

MAKES ABOUT ½ CUP

SWEET-AND-SOUR DIPPING SAUCE

I love the sunset color and piquant flavor of this simple dipping sauce. Made with canned pineapple juice for an extra burst of sweet-and-sour flavor, it tastes wonderful with grilled or fried foods. I love it with fresh raw or steamed vegetables and rice, when I need to round out a quick stir fry. The liquid from a can of pineapple chunks or rings works fine here, if you don't have pineapple juice proper.

⅓ cup pineapple juice

⅓ cup white vinegar or
apple cider vinegar

⅓ cup sugar

1 tablespoon ketchup

1 teaspoon salt

2 tablespoons water

2 teaspoons cornstarch

MAKES ABOUT ¾ CUP

✳ In a medium saucepan, combine the pineapple juice, vinegar, sugar, ketchup, and salt. Stir everything together well. In a small bowl, combine the water and cornstarch and stir until smooth.

✳ Bring the pineapple juice mixture to a gentle boil over medium heat, and cook for 2 minutes, stirring often to dissolve the sugar and mix everything well.

✳ Stir in the cornstarch mixture, watching as the sauce becomes first cloudy and then clear within just a few seconds. Stir well as it thickens to a satiny smooth texture with big bubbles, about 15 seconds more. Remove from the heat, transfer to a bowl, and cool to room temperature. Transfer to a jar and refrigerate for up to 3 days.

(left to right) Tangy Plum Sauce, Sweet-and-Sour Dipping Sauce, Ginger-Soy Dipping Sauce

TANGY PLUM SAUCE

This dip uses bottled plum sauce, widely available in Asian markets and often in supermarkets as well. Made from a traditional salt-preserved plum, it has a marvelously sweet-and-sharp flavor that goes nicely with grilled and fried dishes. You could also use duck sauce, a popular sweet-and-sour dipping sauce which is easy to find. (To brighten the flavor of plain prepared duck sauce, stir in a squeeze of lemon or lime juice or a dash or two of vinegar before serving.)

½ cup prepared Chinese-style plum sauce or duck sauce

1 tablespoon white vinegar or freshly squeezed lemon juice

1 teaspoon light-brown or dark-brown sugar

¼ teaspoon salt

✱ Combine the plum sauce, vinegar, brown sugar, and salt in a medium bowl. Whisk or stir well to dissolve the sugar and salt and mix everything together well.

MAKES ABOUT $^1/_2$ CUP

HOT CHILI OIL

This incendiary condiment graces noodle shop tables throughout Asia and makes a versatile addition to your sauce and seasoning shelf. A simple concoction of coarsely ground red pepper flakes cooked briefly in hot oil, it can be spooned onto noodles or soups, or added to dipping sauces and salad dressings. You can scoop up both flakes and oil, or spoon out only the rust-colored oil. The chiles burn easily during the cooking process, so have a big bowl handy in which to turn out the chili oil as soon as it is ready.

⅓ cup vegetable oil

½ cup coarsely ground red pepper flakes (see Note)

MAKES ABOUT ⅓ CUP

☸ ☸ ☸

NOTE *Red pepper flakes work well in this recipe, but if you adore chili heat and want a stellar version, grind whole dried red chile peppers yourself. Use dried* chiles de arbol *or* chiles japones, *widely available in supermarkets; or small dried red chiles found in Asian markets, often imported from Thailand, Korea, or China. Break off and discard the stem ends, and then transfer the chiles to a small food processor or a blender. Grind until you have small chili flakes and seeds, pulsing the motor as you go. Don't forget to clean your food processor or blender very well.*

☸ ☸ ☸

✳ Place a heatproof medium bowl next to the stove for the finished chili oil.

✳ Heat the oil in a small saucepan over medium heat until it is hot enough to sizzle a red pepper flake on contact. Add the red pepper flakes and stir well. They should bubble and sizzle in a lively way. Continue stirring, and as soon as they have colored just a little, pour the chili oil, including the red pepper flakes, into the bowl.

✳ Let the chili oil cool to room temperature. Transfer to a glass jar and cover tightly. Store at room temperature for up to 1 month.

BROWN SAUCE

This simple sauce is the standard accompaniment to Chinese American–style egg *foo yong*. You can make it up to 2 hours ahead, refrigerate it, and then warm it gently just before serving. Pour it over the hot omelets just before serving them, or offer it on the side in a small bowl or pitcher.

½ cup, plus 2 tablespoons water

2 tablespoons soy sauce

½ teaspoon sugar

½ teaspoon salt

2 teaspoons cornstarch

¼ teaspoon Asian sesame oil

MAKES ABOUT ²/₃ CUP

✳ Combine the ½ cup of water and the soy sauce, sugar, and salt in a small saucepan over medium-high heat. Bring to a rolling boil and stir to dissolve the sugar and salt.

✳ Combine the cornstarch and 2 tablespoons water in a small bowl and stir well. Add to the pan and stir quickly to mix it into the sauce. As soon as the mixture thickens and returns to a boil, remove from the heat, stir in the sesame oil, and set aside. Serve hot or warm.

TOASTED SZECHUAN PEPPERCORNS

These will add more depth to your dishes than regular ground pepper. Toasting heightens their flavor, which provides a rustic kick.

¼ cup raw Szechuan peppercorns

MAKES ABOUT ¹/₃ CUP

✳ To toast the peppercorns, place them in a small, dry skillet over medium heat. Cook, shaking the pan to heat them evenly and well, until they have darkened a little and released their fragrance, about 2 minutes. Transfer to a saucer to cool, and then grind them to a fairly smooth powder. Store in a tightly sealed jar for up to 3 weeks.

CARAMEL GINGER SAUCE

Fresh ginger brightens this simple dessert sauce, which provides a luscious finish to **Five-Spice Poached Pears** (page 165) or bowls of ice cream. If you're making this sauce in advance, know that it may turn grainy after it cools and don't despair. Rewarm it gently on the stove or in a microwave oven, and its smooth texture comes right back.

1 cup heavy (whipping) cream or evaporated milk

10 thin slices fresh ginger

2 cups dark-brown or light-brown sugar

6 tablespoons butter, cut into ½-inch pieces

2 tablespoons light corn syrup

MAKES ABOUT 2 CUPS

✳ Heat the cream in a medium saucepan over medium-high heat until steaming hot. Add the ginger, stir well, remove from the heat, and set aside to steep for 5 minutes.

✳ Add the brown sugar, butter, and corn syrup, and bring to a gentle boil over medium heat. Cook, stirring often, until the butter has melted, the sugar has dissolved, and everything combines and thickens into a smooth, shiny sauce, 8 to 10 minutes. Remove from the heat.

✳ Using a fork, scoop out and discard the slices of ginger. Serve warm. If preparing in advance, set aside to cool completely, and then transfer to a jar or other covered container and refrigerate up to one week. Rewarm gently before serving.

FIRM TOFU

Supermarkets and Asian grocery stores usually carry tofu in an array of textures, from silken to soft to extra firm. Soft tofu can be transformed into sturdy tofu that takes well to stir-frying. Simply press it between two plates long enough to extract some of its water content. The shape will be wonderfully odd after pressing, but the texture will be pleasing and perfect for cooking. Pressing soft tofu will produce half its weight in firm tofu.

1 pound soft or medium tofu

MAKES ABOUT 8 OUNCES VERY FIRM TOFU

✳ Set out two kitchen towels and two dinner plates. Fold one kitchen towel in half and place it on a dinner plate. Place a second kitchen towel over the towel on the dinner plate, opening it up and centering it on the plate.

✳ Cut the block of tofu into four pieces. Place the large tofu pieces in the center of the open towel, about 1 inch apart. Fold the towel in so that the tofu is loosely but firmly enclosed in a cloth packet. Set the plate of tofu in the sink, or in a large rimmed baking pan, so that the liquid to be released by the tofu won't spill onto the countertop. Set the other dinner plate on top of the tofu, and press down gently to balance it. Place a heavy object, such as 4 unopened cans of food, or a full teakettle, on the plate to press down on the soft tofu within.

✳ Let this improvised, low-tech press do its job of pressing water out of the tofu blocks for as little as 30 minutes, or as long as 2 hours. The longer the pressing, the firmer the tofu.

✳ Remove the weights and the top plate, and unwrap the kitchen towel enclosing the tofu. Transfer to a covered container and store in the refrigerator for up to 3 days.

MANDARIN PANCAKES

I love making these simple flatbreads, because they taste wonderful and because they seem difficult but aren't. Step-by-step you simply stir, knead, shape, and roll, and you're a minute or two away from a warm round of tasty bread. Fill pancakes with **Mu Shu Pork** (page 87) or chunks of roast chicken with cucumbers and hoisin sauce. Recruit a partner or a circle of friends to make preparing this recipe extra simple and fun. You can make these ahead and reheat them gently by steaming them or turning each one a few times in a hot, dry skillet just before serving time.

2 cups flour

½ cup boiling water

2 tablespoons Asian sesame oil

MAKES 16 PANCAKES

✳ Pour the flour into a medium bowl and add the boiling water. Quickly and vigorously stir to bring the two ingredients together into a rough dough, using a fork or a wooden spoon.

✳ When the dough is cool enough to touch, gather it up and place it on a lightly floured work surface.

✳ Set a timer and knead the dough until it is tender and smooth, about 10 minutes. Cover with the bowl in which you mixed it or a kitchen towel and set aside to rest for about 15 minutes, or as long as 1 hour.

✳ To divide the dough into 16 pieces, form it first into a 12-inch log. Cut the log into 8 pieces, and then cut each piece in half for a total of 16 pieces of dough. Roll each one into a smooth ball, flatten it into a disk, dab a little sesame oil on top, and then press all the disks together in pairs, sesame-oiled sides in. You'll have 8 little double-layered disks of dough.

✳ On a lightly floured work surface, roll each disk into a thin pancake, 5 to 6 inches in diameter. Aim for roundness, but don't worry if you don't make perfect circles.

✳ To cook the pancakes, heat a large skillet over medium-low heat until hot. Place one double-layer pancake in the center of the pan and cook it for about 1 minute, until it bubbles and puffs up a little. Turn gently and cook about 45 seconds on the other side, until it is tender, but not brittle. Brown spots may or may not show up—don't worry about them either way.

✳ Transfer to a serving plate and find a spot on the side where the two layers are ready to separate from each other. Pull them gently apart, and stack them oiled sides up, covered, while you finish cooking the other 7 pancake pairs.

✳ Serve the pancakes hot or warm. To keep for later use, set aside to cool to room temperature. Wrap them airtight and refrigerate for up to 2 days. Reheat in a skillet the same way you cooked them, or steam them gently until tender and warm.

QUICK & EASY CHINESE MENUS

PICNIC BASKET
✳ Hoisin Shrimp in Lettuce Cups (page 21)
✳ Soy Sauce Chicken Wings (page 27)
✳ Broccoli with Garlic and Ginger (page 127)
   Baguette with cheese and summer sausages
✳ Egg Custard Tartlets (page 162)
   Watermelon slices

BIRTHDAY FEAST
✳ Eight-Treasure Fried Rice (page 138)
✳ Char Shiu Pork (page 98)
✳ Everyday Noodles with Sesame Oil (page 143)
   Birthday cake

SPRING BREAK
✳ Egg Flower Soup (page 38)
✳ Salmon with Ginger and Onions (page 111)
✳ Asparagus with Ginger and Sesame Oil (page 123)
✳ Everyday Rice (page 132)
   Strawberries with sour cream and brown sugar

DUMPLING PARTY
✳ Pot Sticker Dumplings with Ginger-Soy Dipping
   Sauce (page 23)
✳ Won Ton Soup (page 40)
   Edamame beans in the pod

✳ Cool and Tangy Cucumbers (page 126)
✳ Ice cream with Candied Walnuts (page 166)

IT WAS A DARK AND STORMY NIGHT...
✳ Hot and Sour Soup (page 44)
✳ Ham-and-Egg Fried Rice (page 134)
   Peas with butter, salt, and pepper
   Baked Apples

TEA PARTY
✳ Green Onion Pancakes (page 29)
   Cucumber sandwiches
✳ Almond Cookies (page 157)
✳ Egg Custard Tartlets (page 162)
✳ Candied Walnuts (page 166)
   A selection of hot Chinese teas and iced herb teas

VEGETARIAN FEAST
✳ Egg Flower Soup (page 38)
✳ Crisp-fried tofu, served with Sweet-and-Sour Dipping
   Sauce (page 172)
✳ Bok Choy Stir-Fried with Garlic (page 120)
✳ Everyday Noodles with Sesame Oil (page 143)
✳ Five-Spice Poached Pears (page 165) with Caramel
   Ginger Sauce (page 177)

FURTHER READING & COOKING

Alford, Jeffrey, and Nao Duguid. *Hot, Sour, Salty, Sweet: A Culinary Journey through Southeast Asia.* New York: Artisan, 2000.

————. *Seductions of Rice: A Cookbook.* New York: Artisan, 1998.

Bladholm, Linda. *The Asian Grocery Store Demystified.* Los Angeles: Renaissance Books, 1999.

Chen, Pearl Kong, Tien-Chi Chen, and Rose Y. L. Tseng. *Everything You Want to Know about Chinese Cooking.* New York: Barron's, 1983.

Cost, Bruce. *Asian Ingredients: A Guide to the Foodstuffs of China, Japan, Korea, Thailand and Vietnam.* New York: William Morrow, 1998.

Hom, Ken. *Chinese Technique: An Illustrated Guide to the Fundamental Techniques of Chinese Cooking.* New York: Simon & Schuster, 1981.

Kuo, Irene. *Key to Chinese Cooking.* New York: Knopf, 1977.

Leung, Mai. *Dim Sum and Other Chinese Street Food.* New York: Harper & Row, 1982.

Lin, Florence. *Florence Lin's Chinese Regional Cookbook.* New York: Hawthorn Books, 1975.

Lo, Eileen Yin-Fei. *The Chinese Kitchen.* New York: William Morrow, 1999.

Nguyen, Andrea Quynhgiao. *Into the Vietnamese Kitchen: Treasured Foodways, Modern Flavors.* Berkeley: Ten Speed Press, 2006.

O'Connor, Jill. *Sticky, Chewy, Messy, Gooey: Desserts for the Serious Sweet Tooth.* San Francisco: Chronicle Books, 2007.

Oseland, James. *Cradle of Flavor: Home Cooking from the Spice Islands of Indonesia, Malaysia, and Singapore.* New York: W. W. Norton, 2006.

Passmore, Jacki. *Asia, The Beautiful Cookbook.* San Francisco: Collins Publishers, 1998.

Perry, Sara. *Holiday Baking: New and Traditional Recipes for Wintertime Holidays.* San Francisco: Chronicle Books, 2005.

Ross, Rosa Lo-San. *Beyond Bok Choy: A Cook's Guide to Asian Vegetables.* New York: Artisan, 1996.

Sinclair, Kevin. *China, The Beautiful Cookbook.* San Francisco: Collins Publishers, 1998.

Solomon, Charmaine. *The Complete Asian Cookbook.* New York: McGraw-Hill, 1985.

————. *Mastering the Art of Chinese Cooking.* New York: McGraw-Hill, 1984.

Trang, Corrine. *Essentials of Asian Cuisine: Fundamentals and Favorite Recipes.* New York: Simon & Schuster, 2005.

Tropp, Barbara. *China Moon Cookbook.* New York: Workman, 1992.

————. *The Modern Art of Chinese Cooking: Techniques and Recipes.* New York: Hearst Books, 1982.

Wong, S. T. Ting, and Sylvia Schulman. *Madame Wong's Long-Life Chinese Cookbook.* Chicago: Contemporary Books, 1977.

Young, Grace. *The Wisdom of the Chinese Kitchen: Classic Family Recipes for Celebration and Healing.* New York: Simon & Schuster, 1999.

Young, Grace, and Alan Richardson. *The Breath of a Wok: Unlocking the Spirit of Chinese Wok Cooking through Recipes and Lore.* New York: Simon & Schuster, 2004.

Yee, Rhoda. *Chinese Village Cookbook: A Practical Guide to Cantonese Country Cooking.* San Francisco: Yerba Buena Press, 1975.

Yueh, Jean. *The Great Tastes of Chinese Cooking: Contemporary Methods and Menus.* New York: Times Books, 1979.

MAIL-ORDER SOURCES for asian ingredients

ADRIANA'S CARAVAN
43rd Street and Lexington Avenue
New York, NY 10017
phone (800) 316-0820
www.adrianascaravan.com

IMPORT FOOD
P.O. Box 2054
Issaquah, WA 98027
phone (888) 618-8424
fax (425) 687-8413
www.importfood.com

THE ORIENTAL PANTRY
423 Great Road, 2A
Acton, MA 01720
phone (978) 264-4576
fax (781) 275-4506
www.orientalpantry.com

TEMPLE OF THAI
P.O. Box 112
Carroll, IA 51401
phone (877) 811-8773
fax (712) 792-0698
www.templeofthai.com

INDEX